Motion to Reopen in Absentia Order of Removal (No Notice)

Motion to Reopen in Absentia Order of Removal Petition prepared by Immigration Law Firm

Attorney Brian D. Lerner

LAW OFFICES OF
BRIAN D. LERNER
A PROFESSIONAL CORPORATION

ATTORNEY DRAFTED IMMIGRATION PETITIONS

By

Brian D. Lerner

Attorney at Law

Disclaimer and Terms of Use:

Effort has been made to ensure that the information in this book is accurate and complete. However, the author and the publisher do not warrant that this particular petition will mirror or be exactly as your situation. There has not been any attorney-client agreement created by the purchase of this petition or application. No legal advice has occurred. The cases, regulations and/or statutes cited may change at any time without notice.

ISBN: 978-1-948774-97-0

INTRODUCTION

There are a multitude of different immigration petitions and applications. They are complex and full of requirements. Obviously, it would be best to hire an immigration attorney to best prepare the petitions and applications. However, this can certainly cost thousands of dollars.

The next best option is to get a sample of the petition written by an experienced immigration attorney. The samples cost a fraction what would be charged by an immigration attorney. However, while the reader has to alter, amend and change the parts of the sample petition to reflect their actual situation, it is a fantastic roadmap for them to use. If the reader has purchased the entire petition or application, they will have real live samples of cover letters, forms, declarations, affidavits and the necessary exhibits to use. The samples come from real cases and the names of those clients have been redacted to protect the privacy of that person or corporation.

These are petitions and applications that have been drafted by an experienced immigration attorney with over 25 years of experience. Get the benefits of that experience without the costs.

CONTENTS

About the Law Offices of Brian D. Lerner

Brian D. Lerner has been a licensed attorney since 1992 and started the Law Offices of Brian D. Lerner, APC. The law practice consists of Immigration and Nationality Law and everything involved with and regarding immigration which includes citizenship, investment visas, family and employment visas, removal and deportation hearings, appeals, waivers, adjustment, consulate processing and all types of immigration and citizenship matters. Thousands of families have been reunited and/or permitted to stay in the U.S. and/or return to the U.S. because of the successful work of Immigration Attorney Brian D. Lerner.

This law offices handles all types of immigration cases including family based and employment based. Immigration issues range from immigration court proceedings to trying to fix what paralegals may have done that was neither correct nor proper. Foreign nationals must have experience lawyers admitted to practice law.

The Law Offices of Brian D. Lerner, APC, handles cases arising from business visas, work permits, Green Cards, non-immigrant visas, deportation, citizenship, appeals and all areas of immigration. The Law Offices of Brian D. Lerner, APC does EB-5 Investor Visas, H-1B Specialty Occupation, L-1 Intracompany Transferee, E-2 Treaty Investor, E-1 Treaty Trader, O-1 Extraordinary Ability among others. Regarding immigrant visas for the Green Card, the firm does PERM and advanced degree PERM, Family Petitions, and Extraordinary Alien Petitions. In addition to affirmative petitions, the Law Firm represents people in people in deportation and removal hearings, including political asylum, withholding of removal, and convention against torture cases.

Brian D. Lerner has been certified as an expert in Immigration & Nationality Law by the California State Bar, Board of Legal Specialization since 2000 and has been re-certified three times. He now passes on his decades of experience by allowing the Reader, Law Schools, Professors and other Immigration Attorneys to purchase sample petitions on every facet of Immigration Law.

About Motion to Reopen in Absentia Order of Removal

(No Notice)

Motion to Reopen in Absentia Order of Removal (No Notice). This will take place where the absentia order of removal or deportation was entered. A motion to reopen based on lack of proper notice can be filed at any time. Even after a person has left the United States.

FORMS

Notice of Entry of Appearance as Attorney or Representative before the Immigration Court

U.S. Department of Justice
Executive Office for Immigration Review
Immigration Court

OMB#1125-0006

Notice of Entry of Appearance as Attorney or
Representative Before the Immigration Court

(Type or Print)
NAME AND ADDRESS OF REPRESENTED PARTY

(First)	E (Middle Initial)	(Last)
(Number and Street)		(Apt. No.)
Davis (City)	CA (State)	95618 (Zip Code)

ALIEN ("A") NUMBER
(Provide A-number of the party represented in this case.)

098-350-736

Attorney or Representative (please check one of the following):

☒ I am an attorney eligible to practice law in, and a member in good standing of, the bar of the highest court(s) of the following states(s), possession(s), territory(ies), commonwealth(s), or the District of Columbia (use additional space on reverse side if necessary) and I am not subject to any order disbarring, suspending, enjoining, restraining or otherwise restricting me in the practice of law in any jurisdiction (if subject to such an order, do not check this box and explain on reverse).

Full Name of Court **California Supreme Court**   Bar Number (if applicable) **235438**

☐ I am a representative accredited to appear before the Executive Office for Immigration Review as defined in 8 C.F.R. § 1292.1(a)(4) with the following recognized organization:

☐ I am a law student or law graduate of an accredited U.S. law school as defined in 8 C.F.R. § 1292.1(a)(2).

☐ I am a reputable individual as defined in 8 C.F.R. § 1292.1(a)(3).

☐ I am an accredited foreign government official, as defined in 8 C.F.R. § 1291.1(a)(5), from _____ (country).

☐ I am a person who was authorized to practice on December 23, 1952, under 8 C.F.R. § 1292.1(b).

Attorney or Representative (please check one of the following):

☐ I hereby enter my appearance as attorney or representative for, and at the request of, the party named above.

☐ EOIR has ordered the provision of a Qualified Representative for the party named above and I appear in that capacity.

I have read and understand the statements provided on the reverse side of this form that set forth the regulations and conditions governing appearances and representations before the Board of Immigration Appeals. I declare under penalty of perjury under the laws of the United States of America that the foregoing is true and correct.

SIGNATURE OF ATTORNEY OR REPRESENTATIVE	EOIR ID NUMBER	DATE
X	LY310791	04/20/2015

NAME OF ATTORNEY OR REPRESENTATIVE, ADDRESS, FAX & PHONE NUMBERS, & EMAIL ADDRESS

Name: **Christopher**   **A**   **Reed**
       (First)   (Middle Initial)   (Last)

Address: **3233 E. Broadway**
         (Number and Street)

Long Beach	**CA**	**90803**
(City)	(State)	(Zip Code)

Telephone: **(562) 495-0554**   Facsimile: **(562) 608-8672**   Email: **creed@eimmigration.org**

☐ Check here if new address

Form EOIR - 28
Rev. Oct. 2014

APPEARANCES - An appearance shall be filed on a Form EOIR-28 by the attorney or representative appearing in each case before an Immigration Judge (see 8 C.F.R. § 1003.17). When an appearance is made by a person acting in a representative capacity, his/her personal appearance or signature constitutes a representation that, under the provisions of 8 C.F.R. part 1003, he/she is authorized and qualified to represent individuals and will comply with the EOIR Rules of Professional Conduct in 8 C.F.R. § 1003.102. Thereafter, substitution or withdrawal may be permitted upon the approval of the Immigration Judge of a request by the attorney or representative of record in accordance with 8 C.F.R. § 1003.17(b). Please note that appearances for limited purposes are not permitted. See *Matter of Velasquez*, 19 I&N Dec. 377, 384 (BIA 1986). A separate appearance form (Form EOIR-27) must be filed with an appeal to the Board of Immigration Appeals (see 8 C.F.R. § 1003.38(g)). Attorneys and Accredited Representatives (with full accreditation) must first update their address in eRegistry before filing a Form EOIR-28 that reflects a new address.

FREEDOM OF INFORMATION ACT - This form may not be used to request records under the Freedom of Information Act or the Privacy Act. The manner of requesting such records is in 28 C.F.R. §§ 16.1-16.11 and appendices. For further information about requesting records from EOIR under the Freedom of Information Act, see How to File a Freedom of Information Act (FOIA) Request With the Executive Office for Immigration Review, available on EOIR's website at http://www.justice.gov/eoir.

PRIVACY ACT NOTICE - The information requested on this form is authorized by 8 U.S.C. §§ 1229(a), 1362 and 8 C.F.R. § 1003.17 in order to enter an appearance to represent a party before the Immigration Court. The information you provide is mandatory and required to enter an appearance. Failure to provide the requested information will result in an inability to represent a party or receive notice of actions in a proceeding. EOIR may share this information with others in accordance with approved routine uses described in EOIR's system of records notice, EOIR-001, Records and Management Information System, 69 Fed. Reg. 26,179 (May 11, 2004), or its successors and EOIR-003, Practitioner Complaint-Disciplinary Files, 64 Fed. Reg. 49237 (September 1999).

CASES BEFORE EOIR - Automated information about cases before EOIR is available by calling (800) 898-7180 or (240) 314-1500.

FURTHER INFORMATION - For further information, please see the *Immigration Court Practice Manual*, which is available on the EOIR website at *www.justice.gov/eoir*.

ADDITIONAL INFORMATION:

Form EOIR - 28
Rev. Oct. 2014

Alien's Change of Address Form/Immigration Court

U.S. Department of Justice
Executive Office for Immigration Review
Immigration Court

OMB# 1125-0004

Alien's Change of Address Form/
Immigration Court

If you move or change your phone number, the law requires you to file this Change of Address Form with the Immigration Court. You must file this form within five (5) working days of a change in your address or phone number. You will only receive notification as to the time, date, and place of hearing or other official correspondence at the address which you provide. Changes in address or telephone numbers communicated through any means except this form, e.g., pleadings, motion papers, correspondence, telephone calls, applications for relief, etc. will not be recognized and the address information and record will remain unchanged.

Failure to appear at any hearing before an Immigration Judge, when notice of that hearing or other official correspondence was served on you or sent to the address you provided, may result in one or more of the following actions:

- If you are not already detained, you may be taken into custody by the Department of Homeland Security (DHS) and held for further action; and

If you are in *removal* proceedings:	If you are in *deportation* proceedings:	If you are in *exclusion* proceedings:
Your hearing may be held in your absence under Section 240 of the Immigration and Nationality Act (INA) (1995), and an order of removal may be entered against you. Furthermore, you may become ineligible for the following forms of relief from removal for a period of 10 years after the date of the entry of the final order: 1. Voluntary Departure as provided for in Section 240B of the INA; 2. Cancellation of Removal as provided for in Section 240A of the INA; 3. Adjustment of Status or Change of Status as provided for in Section(s) 245, 248, or 249 of the INA.	Your hearing may be held in your absence under Section 242B of the Immigration and Nationality Act (INA) (1995), and an order of deportation may be entered against you. Furthermore, you may become ineligible for the following forms of relief from deportation for a period of 5 years after the date of the entry of the final order: 1. Voluntary Departure as provided for in Section 242(b) of the INA (1995); 2. Suspension of Deportation or Voluntary Departure as provided for in Section 244 of the INA (1995); 3. Adjustment of Status or Change of Status as provided for in Section(s) 245, 248, or 249 of the INA (1995).	Your application for admission to the United States may be considered withdrawn, and your hearing may be held in your absence and an order of exclusion and deportation entered against you.

Name: MEZA AVENIO, Amorico Ernesto   *Alien Number: A* 098-350-736

My **OLD** address was:	My **NEW** address is:
("In care of" other person, if any)	("In care of" other person, if any)
▮▮▮▮▮▮▮▮▮▮▮▮▮▮▮▮	▮▮▮▮▮▮▮ ▮▮▮▮
(Number, Street, Apartment)	(Number, Street, Apartment)
Davis CA 95618	Davis CA 95618
(City, State and ZIP Code)	(City, State and ZIP Code)
USA	USA
(Country, if other than U.S.)	(Country, if other than U.S.)
	▮▮▮▮▮▮▮▮
	(New Telephone Number)

✍ **SIGN HERE** ➡ X _____   _4/15/15_
                          Signature   *Date*

PROOF OF SERVICE (You Must Complete This)

I _Christopher A. Reed_____ mailed or delivered a copy of this Change of Address Form on
      (Name)
_4/24/15_ to the Office of the Chief Counsel for the DHS (U.S. Immigration and Customs Enforcement-ICE) at
  (Date)
606 S, Olive Street, 8th Floor   Los Angeles, CA 90014.
          (Number and Street) City, State, Zip Code)

✍ **SIGN HERE** ➡ X _____
                          Signature

Form EOIR - 33/IC
Revised October 2013

4117

MAILING INSTRUCTIONS

1) Copy the completed form and mail or deliver it to the Office of the Chief Counsel DHS-ICE at the address you inserted in the PROOF OF SERVICE. The PROOF OF SERVICE certifies that you provided a copy of the form to DHS.
2) Fold the page at the dotted lines marked "Fold Here" so that the address is visible.
   (IMPORTANT: Make sure the address section is visible after folds are made.)
3) Secure the folded form by stapling along the open end marked "Fasten Here."
4) Place appropriate postage stamp in the area marked "Place Stamp Here."
5) Write in your return address in the area marked "PUT YOUR ADDRESS HERE."
6) Mail the original form to the Immigration Court whose address is printed below.

Fold Here

- -

PUT YOUR ADDRESS HERE

Law Offices of Brian D. Lerner,
APC
3233 E. Broadway
Long Beach, CA 90803

| Place |
| Stamp |
| Here |

U.S. Department of Justice

606 S. Olive Street, 15th
FL
Los Angeles, CA 90014

- -

Fold Here

Form EOIR - 33/IC
Revised October 2013

Fasten Here

Motion to Reopen Cover Letter

Brian D. Lerner (Bar No. 158536)
Christopher A. Reed (Bar No. 235438)
Law Offices of Brian D. Lerner, APC
3233 E. Broadway
Long Beach, CA 90803
Telephone: (562) 495-0554
Facsimile: (562) 608-8672

Attorneys for Respondent

UNITED STATES DEPARTMENT OF JUSTICE

EXECUTIVE OFFICE FOR IMMIGRATION REVIEW

IMMIGRATION COURT

LOS ANGELES, CALIFORNIA

In the Matter of:

███████████████████   File No: ██████████

Respondent,

In Removal Proceedings.

Immigration Judge: Next Hearing: N/A

**MOTION TO REOPEN, MOTION TO RESCIND IN ABSENTIA ORDER OF REMOVAL
AND AUTOMATIC STAY OF REMOVAL
(NO NOTICE)**

TABLE OF CONTENTS

Removal Proceeding Attorney's Brief

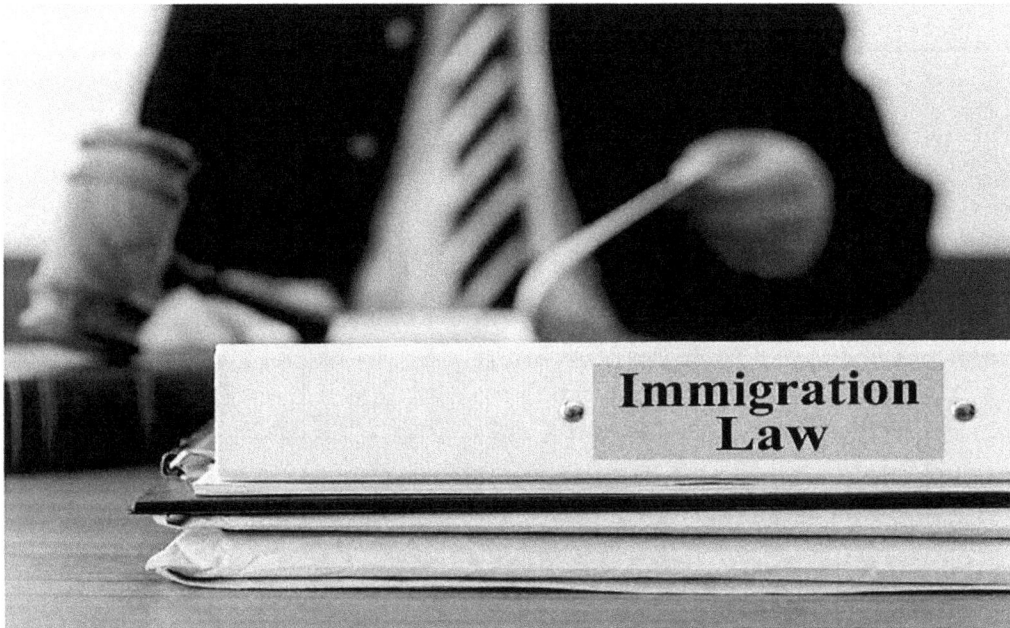

Brian D. Lerner (Bar No. 158536)
Christopher A. Reed (Bar No. 235438)
Law Offices of Brian D. Lerner, APC
3233 E. Broadway
Long Beach, CA 90803
Telephone: (562) 495-0554
Facsimile: (562) 608-8672

Attorneys for Respondent

UNITED STATES DEPARTMENT OF JUSTICE

EXECUTIVE OFFICE FOR IMMIGRATION REVIEW

IMMIGRATION COURT

LOS ANGELES, CALIFORNIA

In the Matter of:

███████████████████   File No: ███████████

Respondent,

In Removal Proceedings.

Pursuant to section 240(b)(5)(C) of the Immigration and Nationality Act (hereinafter "INA" or "Act"), Respondent, through undersigned counsel, hereby moves the Immigration Court to reopen his case and rescind its in absentia order of removal dated October 17, 2008. The filing of this motion shall automatically stay Respondent's removal pending disposition of this motion by the Court. *Id.*

I.
JURISDICTION AND VENUE

Pursuant to section 240(b)(5)(C)(ii) of the Act, an in absentia order of removal may be rescinded upon a motion to reopen filed at any time if the alien demonstrates that he or she did not receive proper notice. *See also* 8 C.F.R. § 1003(b)(4)(ii); *Matter of Haim,* 19 I&N Dec. 641

(BIA 1988); *Matter of Guzman,* I&N Dec. 722 (BIA 1999). Further, an immigration judge may

upon his or her own motion at any time reopen or reconsider any case in which he or she has

made a decision, unless jurisdiction is vested with the Board of Immigration Appeals (hereinafter

"BIA" or "Board"). 8 C.F.R. § 1003.23(b)(1).

A motion to reopen should be filed with the Immigration Court having administrative

control over the Record of Proceedings. *Id.* at § 1003.23(b)(1)(ii). Typically, this is where the in

absentia order of removal was entered. In the present case, Respondent's in absentia order of

removal was entered by the Immigration Court in Los Angeles, California. Therefore,

Respondent's motion is properly before this Court.

II.
SUMMARY OF RELEVANT FACTS

1. Respondent is a 37-year-old married male, native and citizen of Peru. Tabs B-C.

2. Respondent last entered the United States without inspection at or near Hidalgo, Texas on
   or about October 15, 2004. Tab A and K.

3. On or about October 19, 2004, Respondent was apprehended by Border Patrol and
   removal proceedings were initiated against him with service of a Notice to Appear
   (hereinafter "NTA"). Tabs K-L.

4. Respondent was ordered to appear in court on November 19, 2004 at 1:00 p.m. at ▮▮▮▮
   ▮▮▮▮▮▮▮▮▮▮▮▮▮▮▮▮▮▮▮. Tab K. However, Respondent's
   NTA was not filed by the Department of Homeland Security (hereinafter "DHS") with the
   Los Angeles Immigration Court until June 24, 2008, nearly four years later. Tab K. At
   the same time, DHS moved to change venue from Los Angeles, California to San
   Francisco, CA. Tab M.

5. On July 7, 2008, the Court sent Respondent notice of his initial MASTER hearing scheduled for July 25, 2008. Tab N. That notice was returned to the Immigration Court on July 18, 2014 by the U.S. Postal Service as undeliverable. Tab N.

6. On July 25, 2008, the Court resent Respondent notice of his initial MASTER hearing, now scheduled for October 17, 2008. Tab O. That notice was returned to the Immigration Court on August 8, 2014 by the U.S. Postal Service, also as undeliverable. Tab O.

7. On October 17, 2008, Respondent was ordered removed in absentia by the Immigration Court in Los Angeles, California. Tab P. However, as discussed below, Respondent did not receive notice of his hearings because they were sent to an incorrect address, an address that does not exist. Tabs A and Q.

8. On June 13, 2011, Respondent married ███████████████████, a U.S. citizen. Tabs D-E. Respondent and his wife have two U.S. citizen children together; 10-month old ████████ and 4-year-old ████████████████ Tab F.

9. On March 20, 2014, Respondent's wife filed an I-130, Petition for Alien Relative, with U.S. Citizenship and Immigration Services (hereinafter "USCIS" or "Service") on his behalf. Tab G. Respondent and his wife are scheduled to be interviewed by the Service on April 28, 2015. Tab G.

III.
THIS COURT SHOULD REOPEN RESPONDENT'S CASE PURSUANT TO SECTION 240(b)(5)(C)(ii) OF THE ACT

A. Initiation And Notice Of Removal Proceedings.

Section 239(a)(1) of the Act provides:

> In removal proceedings under section 240, written notice (in this section referred to as a "notice to appear") shall be given in person to the alien (or, if personal

service is not practicable, through service by mail to the alien or to the alien's counsel of record, if any) specifying the following:

(A) The nature of the proceedings against the alien.

(B) The legal authority under which the proceedings are conducted.

(C) The acts or conduct alleged to be in violation of law.

(D) The charges against the alien and the statutory provisions alleged to have been violated.

(E) The alien may be represented by counsel and the alien will be provided (i) a period of time to secure counsel under subsection (b)(1) and (ii) a current list of counsel prepared under subsection (b)(2).

(F) (i) The requirement that the alien must immediately provide (or have provided) the Attorney General with a written record of an address and telephone number (if any) at which the alien may be contacted respecting proceedings under section 240.

(ii) The requirement that the alien must provide the Attorney General immediately with a written record of any change of the alien's address or telephone number.

(iii) The consequences under section 240(b)(5) of failure to provide address and telephone information pursuant to this subparagraph.

(G) (i) The time and place at which the proceedings will be held.

(ii) The consequences under section 240(b)(5) of the failure, except under exceptional circumstances, to appear at such proceedings.

See also 8 C.F.R. §§ 1239; 1003.14; 1003.15.

Similarly, section 239(a)(2)(A) of the Act provides:

In removal proceedings under section 240, in the case of any change or postponement in the time and place of such proceedings, subject to subparagraph (B) a written notice shall be given in person to the alien (or, if personal service is not practicable, through service by mail to the alien or to the alien's counsel of record, if any) specifying-

(i) the new time or place of the proceedings, and

(ii) the consequences under section 240(b)(5) of failing, except under exceptional circumstances, to attend such proceedings.

See also 8 C.F.R § 1003.18.

Finally, section 239(c) of the Act provides:

> Service by mail under this section shall be sufficient if there is proof of attempted delivery to the last address provided by the alien in accordance with subsection (a)(1)(F).

B.   Failure To Appear And Lack Of Notice.

Section 240(b)(5)(A) of the Act provides:

> Any alien who, after written notice required under paragraph (1) or (2) of section 239(a) has been provided to the alien or the alien's counsel of record, does not attend a proceeding under this section, shall be ordered removed in absentia if the Service establishes by clear, unequivocal, and convincing evidence that the written notice was so provided and that the alien is removable (as defined in subsection (e)(2)). The written notice by the Attorney General shall be considered sufficient for purposes of this subparagraph if provided at the most recent address provided under section 239(a) (1)(F).

See also 8 C.F.R. § 1003.26. However, section 240(b)(5)(C)(ii) of the Act provides that an in

absentia order of removal may be rescinded:

> *upon a motion to reopen filed at any time if the alien demonstrates that the alien did not receive notice in accordance with paragraph (1) or (2) of section 239(a) or the alien demonstrates that the alien was in Federal or State custody and the failure to appear was through no fault of the alien.*

In *Matter of G-Y-R-*, 23 I&N Dec. 181 (BIA 2001), the Board of Immigration Appeals

(hereinafter "BIA" or "Board") held than when an alien fails to appear at removal proceedings

for which notice of the hearing was served by mail, an in absentia order may only be entered

where the alien has received, or can be charged with receiving, a Notice to Appear (Form I-862)

informing the alien of the statutory address obligations associated with removal proceedings and of the consequences of failing to provide a current address, pursuant to section 239(a)(1)(F) of the Act.

In *G-Y-R-*, the respondent was a citizen and alien of El Salvador who had filed for asylum in 1982. *Id.* at 182. In 1997, the Service mailed an asylum interview appointment notice to the last address provided by the respondent but the respondent did not appear for her scheduled interview. *Id.* On July 7, 1997, the Service sent to the respondent, by certified mail, a Notice to Appear (Form I-862) for a removal hearing scheduled for September 30, 1997. *Id.* The respondent did not receive the Notice to Appear because it was returned to the Service by the Postal Service. *Id.* In determine whether an in absentia order was appropriate and whether the respondent could be charged with receiving the Notice to Appear, the Board noted that the question was what constitutes a section 239(a)(1)(F) address and concluded that an alien cannot provide a "section 239(a)(1)(F)" address (or "have provided" it and therefore not need to change it) unless the alien has been advised to do so. *Id.* at 187. Accordingly, the Board held that entry of an in absentia order of removal was inappropriate where the record reflected that the respondent did not receive, or could not be charged with receiving, the Notice to Appear that was served by certified mail at an address obtained from documents filed with the Immigration and Naturalization Service several years earlier. *Id.* at 192.

Further, in *Matter of M-R-A-*, 24 I&N Dec. 665 (BIA 2008), the Board held that where a Notice to Appear or Notice of Hearing is properly addressed and sent by regular mail, as opposed to certified mail, according to normal office procedures, there is a presumption of delivery, but it is weaker than the presumption that applies to documents sent by certified mail as set forth in *Matter of Grijalva. See also Salta v. INA*, 314 F.3d 1076, 1079 (9th Cir. 2002)(finding that a sworn affidavit and other circumstantial evidence should ordinarily be sufficient to rebut the presumption of delivery arising from attempted service by regular mail): *Sembiring v. Gonzales*, 499 F.3d 981, 988-89 (9th Cir. 2007)(finding that sufficient evidence may be presented to overcome the presumption of delivery without a sworn affidavit where notice is sent by regular mail). The Board in *M-R-A-* noted that "an inflexible and rigid application of the presumption of delivery" was not appropriate when regular mail is the method of service and therefore, that the court should consider all evidence, both circumstantial and corroborating, when adjudicating a motion to reopen and should consider a variety of factors including, but not limited to: (1) the respondent's declaration; (2) affidavits from family members or other individuals with knowledge of the facts; (3) the respondent's actions upon learning of the in absentia order and whether due diligence was exercised; (4) any prior affirmative application for relief, indicating that the respondent had an incentive to appear; (5) the respondent's previous attendance at Immigration Court hearings; and (6) any other circumstances or evidence indicating possible nonreceipt of notice. *Id. at* 674.

In light of the above factors, the Board in *Matter of M-R-A-* found that the respondent had overcome the presumption of delivery of a Notice of Hearing sent by regular mail given the fact that he submitted affidavits indicating that he did not receive the notice, that he had previously filed an asylum application and appeared for his first removal hearing and that he had exercised due diligence in promptly obtaining counsel and requesting reopening of his proceedings.

C.   **Respondent's Notices of Hearing Were Sent To An Incorrect Address, An Address That Does Not Exist.**

As discussed above, section 240(a)(2)(A) of the Act provides:

> In removal proceedings under section 240, in the case of any change or postponement in the time and place of such proceedings, subject to subparagraph (B) a written notice shall be given in person to the alien (or, if personal service is not practicable, through service by mail to the alien or to the alien's counsel of record, if any) specifying-

(i) the new time or place of the proceedings, and

(ii) the consequences under section 240(b)(5) of failing, except under exceptional circumstances, to attend such proceedings.

See also 8 C.F.R § 1003.18.

Any presumption of notice requires that DHS first establish that the notice was properly addressed. A notice which fails to include an operative part of a properly directed piece of mail is not properly addressed. *See Busquets-Ivars v. Ashcroft*, 333 F.3d 1008 (9th Cir. 2003) (where NTA and Notice of Hearing were sent to address with wrong zip code, *in absentia* order reversed); *Ying Fong v. Ashcroft*, 317 F.Supp.2d 398, 400-03 (S.D.N.Y. 2004); *U.S. v. Montano-Bentancourt*, 151 F.Supp.2d 794 (W.D. Tex. 2001) (where OSC was sent to wrong address and defendant deported in *in absentia* hearing was fundamentally unfair).

In the present case, Respondent was personally served with his NTA, which unbeknownst to him, contained an incorrect address: ███████████████████████ Tabs A, K and Q. Respondent's correct address, which was given to Immigration by his brother prior to his release, was in fact ██████████████████. Tabs A and Q. As a result of this incorrect zip code, Respondent did not receive his Notices of Hearing, which were also sent to ██████████████████████ (an address which does not exist) and subsequently returned by the U.S. Postal Service to the Immigration Court as undeliverable. Tabs A, M-O and Q. Therefore, because Respondent's Notices of Hearing were not properly addressed, he did not receive them and did not receive written notice of the time and place of his proceedings as required by section 240(a)(2)(A) of the Act. For this reason alone, Respondent's case must be reopened.

IV.
CONCLUSION

For the forgoing reasons, Respondent is entitled to reopening of his case as a matter of law. However, even if he were not, this Court should exercise its discretionary power to reopen his case sua sponte given the facts set forth above. Accordingly, Respondent respectfully requests that this Court reopen his case and rescind its in absentia order of removal dated October 17, 2008.

Dated: April 24, 2015

Respectfully submitted,

Christopher A. Reed
Attorney for Respondent

TABS

TAB 'A':

Respondent's Declaration

<u>DECLARATION OF</u> ███████████████████████

I, ███████████████████████, have knowledge of the following facts, and if called to testify thereon I could and would competently testify thereto. I hereby declare as follows:

1. I was born on January 10, 1978 in Cochas, Peru.

2. I entered the United States unlawfully on or about October 15, 2004 and I was arrested by immigration a few days later. I have not left the United States since that time.

3. I married ██████████████████████, a U.S. citizen, on June 13, 2011.

4. ██████ and I have two children together; 10-month-old ████████ and 3-year-old ██████████████

5. Apart from a DUI in 2008 and a conviction for driving without a license in 2011, I have not had any other problems with the law.

6. On March 20, 2014 ██████ filed an immigration petition on my behalf. That petition is currently pending and we are scheduled for an interview on April 28, 2015 in Sacramento, California.

7. When I was arrested by immigration, I used the following address: ██████ ████████████████████████. I planned to stay with my brother and it was he who provided the immigration officer the aforementioned address by phone when I was arrested.

8. After being released, I did not receive any other documents from immigration

9. In 2013, when my son was almost 2-years-old, I decided it was time to fix my immigration problems. I was worried about my wife and son and wanted to make sure that I could provide for them in this country.

10. It was around this time that I found out that I had been ordered deported in 2008.

████████████████████

11. I also found out that my case was not filed until almost 4 years after I entered, that all notices were sent to ████████████████ 95616 instead of ████████████████████ and that they were returned to the court as a result.

12. For these reasons, I ask the court to please reopen my case so that I can fix my immigration problems and stay in the United States with my wife and children.

I declare under penalty of perjury of the laws of the State of California that the above is true and correct to the best of my knowledge.

DATED: 4/15/15

2

DECLARANT'S STATEMENT

The attached declaration has been read to me in the Spanish language, a language in which I am fluent, by the person named in the Interpreter's Statement and Signature below. I understand and attest to contents of the attached declaration.

DATED: 4/15/15

INTERPRETER'S STATEMENT

I, Tanya Stewart, certify that I am fluent in English and the Spanish language. I further certify that I have read the attached declaration to the above-named individual in the above-mentioned language and the above-named individual understood and attested to the contents of the declaration.

DATED: 4.15.15

By: _____
Tanya Stewart

3

TAB 'B':

Respondent's Certificate of Birth

Summarized Translation of Birth Certificate

NAME: ████████████████████████████
      (First)   (Middle)   (First Last Name)   (Second Last Name)

DATE
OF BIRTH: **January 10, 1978**

SEX: **Male**

PLACE OF
BIRTH: DISTRICT: **Cochas**, PROVINCE: **Concepción**, MUNICIPALITY: **Junín**,
COUNTRY: **Republic of Peru**

PARENTS:

FATHER'S
NAME: ████████████████

MOTHER'S
NAME: ████████████████

REGISTRATION
BY: ████████████████

DECLARATION
BY: ████████████████

BIRTH RECORDED
AT: Civil Registry of Cochas, Concepción, Junín, in the file No. 002,
page No. 039, Serial No. 00998814.

DATE OF
REGISTRY: **August 22, 1990**

TEXTUAL
ANNOTATIONS: **Inscription Law 25025**

PLACE AND
DATE OF
THE FAITHFUL
COPY OF THE
ORIGINAL: Cochas, September 24, 2013

THE ABOVE SUMMARIZED TRANSLATION IS A TRUE AND ACCURATE
REPRESENTATION OF AN ORIGINAL, CERTIFIED AND SEALED BIRTH
CERTIFICATE WRITTEN IN THE SPANISH LANGUAGE, WHICH WAS PRESENTED
TO ME BY ITS BEARER ON OCTOBER 12, 2013 FOR THE SOLE PURPOSE OF
TRANSLATING SAID DOCUMENT INTO ENGLISH

Certification by Translator I, Emilio Bejel, certify that I am fluent (conversant)
in the English and Spanish languages, and that the above/attached
document is an accurate translation of the document attached entitled
PARTIDA DE NACIMIENTO (BIRTH CERTIFICATE).

Emilio Bejel
5636 Tufts Street
Davis, CA 95618

Date: October 12, 2013

MUNICIPALIDAD DISTRITAL DE COCHAS

PROVINCIA DE CONCEPCIÓN
-JUNIN-

Nº 105159

OFICINA DE REGISTRO DE ESTADO CIVIL

Partida de Nacimiento

Por la presente CERTIFICA que en el archivo de los Registros Civiles se encuentra inscrita una PARTIDA DE NACIMIENTO, en el libro Nº ......002......., a fojas Nº ....039........, Nº CUI............40968814.... cuyo tenor literal es como sigue:

Nombres: _____ ██████ _____

Apellido Paterno: _____ ███ _____

Apellido Materno: _____ ███ _____

Fecha de Nacimiento: ____ Diez de Enero de Mil Novecientos Setenta y Ocho.

Lugar de Nacimiento: ____ Dist .Cochas, Prov. Concepción, Depto. Junín.

Sexo: ____ Masculino.

Nombre del Padre: ____ Marciano Meza Quintana.

Nombre de la Madre: ____ Epifanía Avenio Vásquez.

Nombre del Declarante: ____ Marciano Meza Quintana.

Fecha de Registro: ____ Veintidós de Agosto de Mil Novecientos Noventa.

Anotaciones textuales: ____ Inscripción Ley 25025.

En fe de lo cual suscriben

El Declarante firmado: ____ ██████ ____

Alcalde: _____

Nombre del Registrador Civil: ____ Elvis Tobal Parado Porras.

ES COPIA FIEL DE SU ORIGINAL

MUNICIPALIDAD DISTRITAL
COCHAS - CONCEPCIÓN - JUNIN

Elvis Tobal Parado Porras
JEFE DE OFICINA DE REGISTRO CIVIL
DNI 40981014

Cochas, 24 de Setiembre del 201 3

MUNICIPALIDAD DISTRITAL DE COCHAS

REGISTRO DEL ESTADO CIVIL

CERTIFICA: Que la presente copia de

fojas vuelta es fiel a su original

Cochas 24 de SETIEMBRE de 2013

MUNICIPALIDAD DISTRITAL
COCHAS - CONCEPCIÓN - JUNIN

Elvis Isaí Parado Porras
JEFE OFICINA DE REGIST. DE CIVIL
DNI. 43698574

RENIEC

15328

EL REGISTRO NACIONAL DE IDENTIFICACIÓN y ESTADO CIVIL, Señe que la firma que aparece en el presente documento pertenece al Jefe de la Oficina de Registros de Estado Civil de la

Presentado de COCHAS CONCEPCION
al ELVIS PARADO PORRAS

Janet Vidal Cabezas
01 OCT. 2013

APOSTILLE
(Convention de la Haye du 5 octobre 1961)

1. País / Country REPÚBLICA DEL PERÚ

   El presente documento público / This public document

2. ha sido firmado por / has been signed by JANET M. VIDAL CABEZAS

3. quién actúa en calidad de / acting in the capacity of REGISTRADOR

4. y está revestido del sello / timbre de / bears the seal / stamp of REGISTRO NACIONAL DE IDENTIFICACIÓN Y ESTADO CIVIL- RENIEC

   Certificado / Certified

5. en / at SEDE CENTRAL - LIMA   6. el / the 03/10/2013

7. por / by MINISTERIO DE RELACIONES EXTERIORES

8. bajo el número / Nº MRE605139120227134679

9. Sello/timbre / Seal/stamp   10. Firma / Signature

Narvaez Mendoza Edwin
Dirección General de Política Consular
MINISTERIO DE RELACIONES EXTERIORES

Serie -03 Nº 949540   www.rree.gob.pe

TAB 'C':

Respondent's Passport

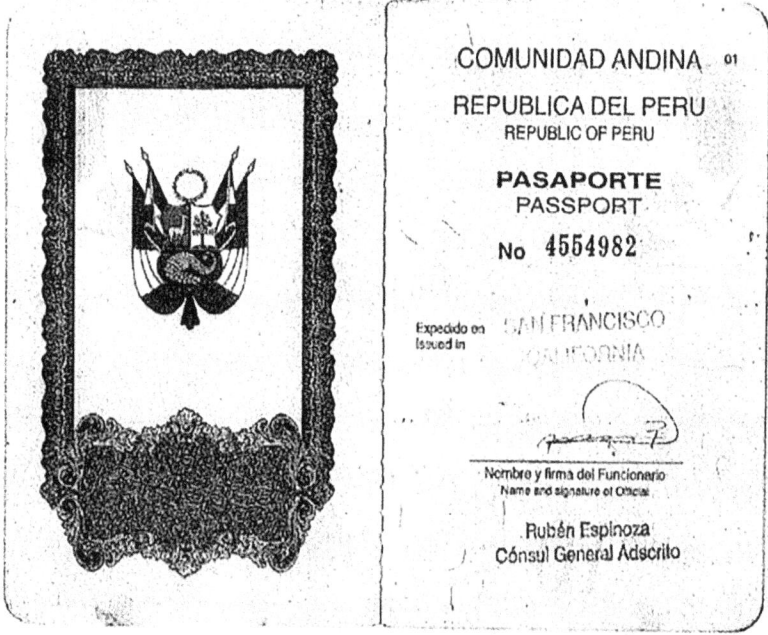

COMUNIDAD ANDINA   01

REPUBLICA DEL PERU
REPUBLIC OF PERU

PASAPORTE
PASSPORT

No 4554982

Expedido en   SAN FRANCISCO
Issued in   CALIFORNIA

_____
Nombre y firma del Funcionario
Name and signature of Official

Rubén Espinoza
Cónsul General Adscrito

OBSERVACIONES
Observations

REPUBLICA DEL PERU

PASAPORTE

PASAPORTE Nº · PASSPORT Nº
4554982

APELLIDOS · SURNAMES

NOMBRES · GIVEN NAMES

SEXO · SEX
M

NACIONALIDAD · NATIONALITY
PERUANA

DOCUMENTO DE IDENTIDAD Nº
10604023

LUGAR DE NACIMIENTO · PLACE OF BIRTH
JUNIN

FECHA DE NACIMIENTO · DATE OF BIRTH
10 ENE 1978

FECHA DE EMISION · DATE OF ISSUE
04 MAY 2009

FECHA DE VENCIMIENTO · DATE OF EXPIRY
04 MAY 2014

FIRMA DEL TITULAR · HOLDER'S SIGNATURE

<<<<<<<<<<

4554982<<5PER7801103M1405048<<<<<<<<<<<<<<06

TAB 'D':

Respondent's License, Certificate and Marriage

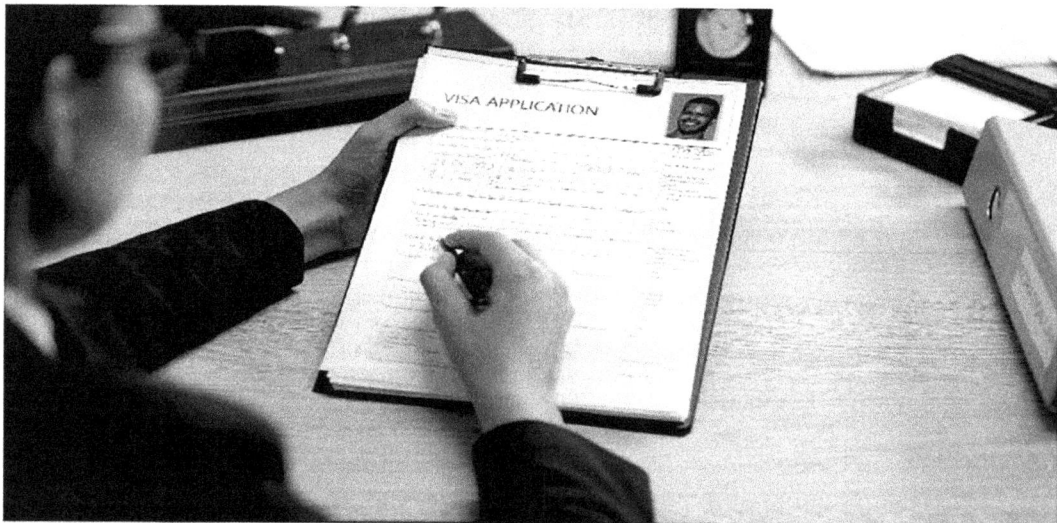

STATE OF CALIFORNIA
CERTIFICATION OF VITAL RECORD

COUNTY OF YOLO
WOODLAND, CALIFORNIA 95695

LICENSE AND CERTIFICATE OF MARRIAGE

4 2 0 1 1 5 7 0 0 0 2 4 6

MORAN-VOGT

10/15/1989 CALIFORNIA 0

CALIFORNIA 95618

CALIFORNIA

CALIFORNIA

01/10/1978 PERU 0

DAVIS CALIFORNIA 95618

MARCIAL GUILLERMO MEZA QUINTANA PERU

PERU

09/25/2011 08/23/2011 Freddie Oakley

11-0000239-00 YOLO P.O. BOX 1130, WOODLAND, CA 95776

AMELIA MEZA

MARK SHEN

06-13-2011 DAVIS YOLO

SPIRITUALIST

REV. DREW L. VOGT REVEREND

4530 18TH ST SAN FRANCISCO, CA 94114

EMILY FRANCES MEZA

Freddie Oakley

TAB 'E':

Respondent's Wife U.S. Passport

PASSPORT
United States of America
AmericanAirlines
AA 72 81 27

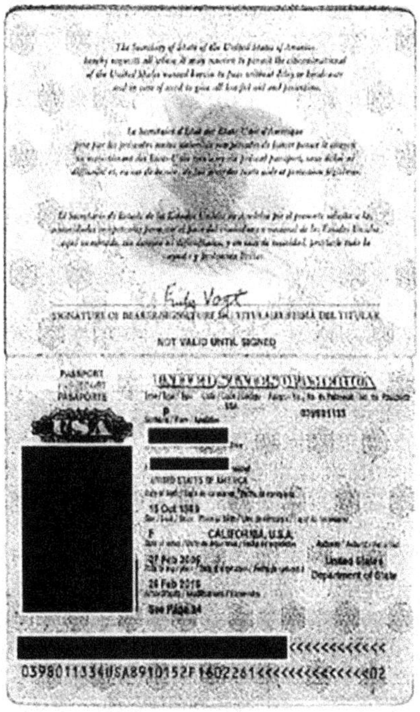
NOT VALID UNTIL SIGNED
UNITED STATES OF AMERICA
USA

TAB 'F':

Respondent's Children U.S. Birth Certificate

COUNTY OF YOLO

WOODLAND, CALIFORNIA 95695

CERTIFICATE OF LIVE BIRTH
STATE OF CALIFORNIA
USE BLACK INK ONLY

1201457001070

LOCAL REGISTRATION NUMBER

1A. NAME OF CHILD - FIRST	1B. MIDDLE	1C. LAST
2. SEX FEMALE	3A. THIS BIRTH SINGLE	3B. IF MULTIPLE THIS CHILD 1ST 2ND ETC	4A. DATE OF BIRTH - MO/DAY/CCYY 06/23/2014	4B. HOUR - 24 HOUR CLOCK TIME 0056
5A. PLACE OF BIRTH - NAME OF HOSPITAL OR FACILITY SUTTER DAVIS HOSPITAL	5B. STREET ADDRESS - STREET AND NUMBER OR LOCATION 2000 SUTTER PLACE	
5C. CITY DAVIS	5D. COUNTY YOLO	
6A. NAME OF FATHER/PARENT - FIRST	6B. MIDDLE	6C. LAST	7. BIRTHPLACE STATE/COUNTRY PERU	8. DATE OF BIRTH - MO/DAY/CCYY 01/10/1978
9A. NAME OF MOTHER/PARENT - FIRST	9B. MIDDLE	9C. LAST - BIRTH NAME	10. BIRTHPLACE STATE/COUNTRY CA	11. DATE OF BIRTH - MO/DAY/CCYY 10/15/1989
12A. I CERTIFY THAT THE PERSONAL INFORMATION PROVIDED ON THIS CERTIFICATE IS TRUE AND CORRECT TO THE BEST OF MY KNOWLEDGE	12B. PARENT OR OTHER INFORMANT - SIGNATURE	13. RELATIONSHIP TO CHILD PARENT	12C. DATE SIGNED - MO/DAY/CCYY 06/24/2014
14. I CERTIFY THAT THIS CHILD WAS BORN ALIVE AT THE PLACE AND TIME AND ON THE DATE STATED	15A. ATTENDANT - SIGNATURE	16. LICENSE NUMBER 2055	15. DATE SIGNED - MO/DAY/CCYY 06/24/2014
16D. TYPED NAME, TITLE AND MAILING ADDRESS OF ATTENDANT RACHEL BALLESTER, CNM, 2000 SUTTER PL DAVIS 95616, DAVIS			
17. DATE OF DEATH - MO/DAY/CCYY	18. STATE FILE NUMBER	19. LOCAL REGISTRAR - SIGNATURE CONSTANCE J. CALDWELL, MD	20. DATE ACCEPTED FOR REGISTRATION - MO/DAY/CCYY 06/30/2014

STATE OF CALIFORNIA
CERTIFICATION OF VITAL RECORD

COUNTY OF YOLO
WOODLAND, CALIFORNIA 95695

CERTIFICATE OF LIVE BIRTH
STATE OF CALIFORNIA
USE BLACK INK ONLY

1201157000917

MALE	SINGLE	06/20/2011	0622

SUTTER DAVIS HOSPITAL — 2000 SUTTER PLACE

DAVIS — YOLO

PERU — 01/10/1978

CA — 10/15/1989

MOTHER — 06/21/2011

NMW1768 — 06/21/2011

JENNIFER TAYLOR, CNM, 2000 SUTTER PLACE, DAVIS

CHRISTIAN SANDROCK, MD, MPH — 06/24/2011

TAB 'G':

I-130 Receipt Notice and Interview Notice

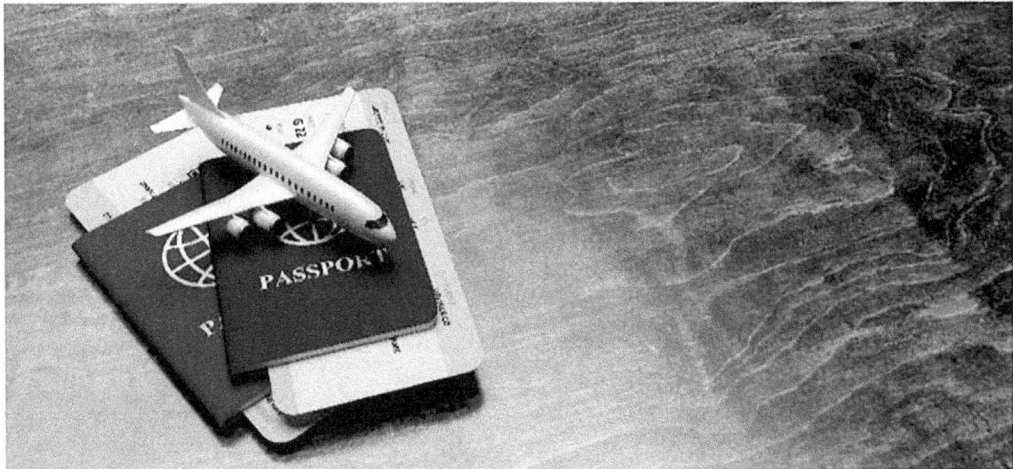

Department of Homeland Security
U.S. Citizenship and Immigration Serv

Form I-797C, Notice of Action

THIS NOTICE DOES NOT GRANT ANY IMMIGRATION STATUS OR BENEFIT.

NOTICE TYPE		NOTICE DATE	
Receipt		March 22, 2014	
CASE TYPE		USCIS ALIEN NUMBER	
I-130, Petition for Alien Relative			
RECEIPT NUMBER	RECEIVED DATE		PAGE
LIN1490429093	March 20, 2014		1 of 1
PRIORITY DATE	PREFERENCE CLASSIFICATION		DATE OF BIRTH
March 20, 2014	201 B INA SPOUSE OF USC		October 15, 1989

PAYMENT INFORMATION:

███████████████

C/O BRIAN D. LERNER LAW OFFICES OF BRIAN D LERNE
3233 E BROADWAY
LONG BEACH, CA 90803

Application/Petition Fee:	$420.00
Biometrics Fee:	$0.00
Total Amount Received:	$420.00
Total Balance Due:	$0.00

APPLICANT/PETITIONER NAME AND MAILING ADDRESS

The I-130, Petition for Alien Relative has been received by our office for the following beneficiaries and is in process:

Name	Date of Birth	Country of Birth	Class (If Applicable)
██████████	1/10/1978	PERU	

Please verify your personal information listed above and immediately notify the USCIS National Customer Service Center at the phone number listed below if there are any changes.

Please note that if a priority date is printed on this notice, the priority does not reflect earlier retained priority dates.

If you have questions about possible immigration benefits and services, filing information, or USCIS forms, please call the USCIS National Customer Service Center (NCSC) at **1-800-375-5283**. If you are hearing impaired, please call the NCSC TDD at **1-800-767-1833**. Please also refer to the USCIS website: www.uscis.gov.

If you have any questions or comments regarding this notice or the status of your case, please contact our customer service number.

You will be notified separately about any other case you may have filed.

USCIS Office Address:	**USCIS Customer Service Number:**
USCIS	(800)375-5283
Nebraska Service Center	ATTORNEY COPY
P.O. Box 82521	
Lincoln, NE 68501-2521	

Department of Homeland Security
U.S. Citizenship and Immigration Services

Form I-797C, Notice of Action

THIS NOTICE DOES NOT GRANT ANY IMMIGRATION STATUS OR BENEFIT.

REQUEST FOR APPLICANT TO APPEAR FOR INTERVIEW			NOTICE DATE April 9 2015
CASE TYPE FORM I-130 PETITION FOR ALIEN RELATIVE			USCIS A# A98350736
APPLICATION NUMBER LIN1490429093	Received date 03/20/2014	PRIORITY DATE 03/20/2014	PAGE 1 of 1

APPLICANT NAME AND MAILING ADDRESS

Americo E. Meza Avenio
c/o: Brian D. Lerner
3233 E. Broadway
Long Beach, CA 90803

You are hereby notified to appear for the interview appointment, as scheduled below, for the completion of your Form I-130, Petition for Alien Relative and any supporting applications or petitions. *Failure to appear for this interview and/or failure to bring the below listed items will result in the denial of your petition* (8 CFR 103.2(b)(13)).

Who should come with you?
* If your eligibility is based on your marriage, your husband or wife must come with you to the interview.
* If you do not speak English fluently, you should bring an interpreter.
* Your attorney or authorized representative may come with you to the interview.
* If your eligibility is based on a parent/child relationship and the child is a minor, the petitioning parent and the child must appear for the interview.

NOTE : Every adult (over 18 years of age) who comes to the interview must bring Government issued photo identification, such as a driver's license or ID card, in order to enter the building and to verify his/her identity at the time of the interview. You do not need to bring your children unless otherwise instructed. Please be on time, but do not arrive more than 45 minutes early. We may record or videotape your interview.

YOU MUST BRING THE FOLLOWING ITEMS WITH YOU:

* This Interview Notice and your Government issued photo identification.
* Any immigration related documentation ever issued to you, including any Employment Authorization Document (EAD) and any Authorization for Advance Parole (Form I-512).
* Your Birth Certificate.
* Your petitioner's Birth Certificate and your petitioner's evidence of United States Citizenship or Lawful Permanent Resident Status.
* If you have children, bring a Birth Certificate for each child.
* If your eligibility is based on your marriage, in addition to your spouse coming to the interview with you, bring:
  * A certified copy of your Marriage Document issued by the appropriate civil authority.;
  * Your spouse's Birth Certificate and your spouse's evidence of United States Citizenship or Lawful Permanent Resident Status.;
  * If either you or your spouse were ever married before, all divorce decrees/death certificates for each prior marriage/spouse;
  * Birth certificates for all children of this marriage, and custody papers for your children and for your spouse's children not living with you.
* Supporting evidence of your relationship, such as copies of any documentation regarding joint assets or liabilities you and your spouse may have together.
* This may include: tax returns, bank statements, insurance documents (car, life, health), property documents (car, house, etc), rental agreements, utility bills, credit cards, contracts, leases, photos, correspondence and/or other documents you feel may substantiate your relationship.
* Original and copy of each supporting document that you submitted with your petition. Otherwise, we may keep your originals for our records.
* A certified English translation for each foreign language documents. The translator must certify that s/he is fluent in both languages, and that the translation in its entirety is complete and accurate.

YOU MUST APPEAR FOR THIS INTERVIEW. If an emergency, such as your own illness or a close relative's hospitalization prevents you from appearing, contact this office at the below listed address as soon as possible. Please be advised that Rescheduling will delay processing of your application/petition, and may require some steps to be repeated. It may also affect your eligibility for other Immigration Benefits while this application is pending.

CURRENT POLICY PROHIBITS THE USE OF CAMERAS OR CAMERA PHONES IN THIS FACILITY. PLEASE DO NOT BRING THESE ITEMS WITH YOU, AS YOU MAY BE DENIED BUILDING ENTRY.

If you have any questions or comments regarding this notice or the status of your case, please contact our office at the below address or customer service number. You will be notified separately about any other cases you may have filed.

PLEASE COME TO:	ON: April 28, 2015
U.S. Citizenship and Immigration Services	AT: 9:45 am
650 Capitol Mall	
2nd Floor, Room 2-220	
Sacramento, CA 95814	

www.uscis.gov

If this is an interview or biometrics appointment notice, please see the back of this notice for important information.   Form I-797C 07/11/14 Y

TAB 'H':

Respondent's California Criminal History Information (CALDOJ)

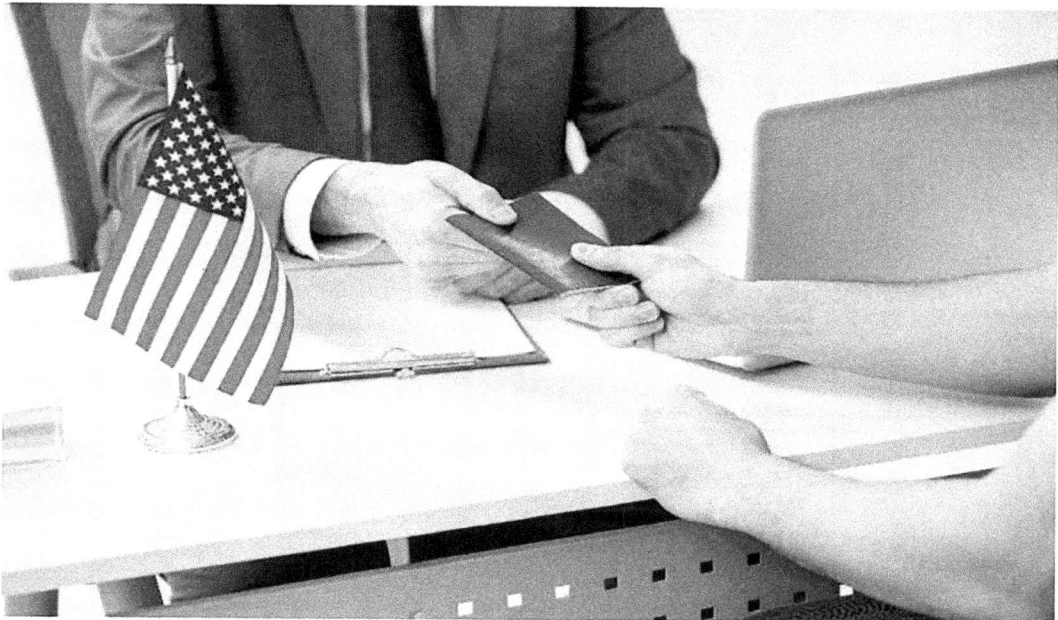

KAMALA D. HARRIS
Attorney General

State of California
DEPARTMENT OF JUSTICE

BUREAU OF CRIMINAL INFORMATION AND ANALYSIS
P.O. Box 903417
SACRAMENTO, CA 94203-4170

January 19, 2015

AMERICO MEZA AVENIO
4735 COWELL BLVD
DAVIS, CA 95618

RE: California Criminal History Information

Dear Applicant:

This is in response to your record review request concerning the existence of a California criminal history record maintained in the files of the Department of Justice's Bureau of Criminal Information and Analysis. Your fingerprints did identify to an existing California criminal history record and a copy of that record is enclosed. If you wish to challenge the accuracy or completeness of your record, please complete and return the enclosed form (BCIA 8706) and supporting documentation to the address noted above.

Pursuant to California Penal Code section 11121, the purpose of a record review request is to afford an individual with a copy of their record and to refute any erroneous or inaccurate information contained therein. The intent is not to be used for licensing, certification or employment purposes.

Additionally, California Penal Code sections 11125, 11142, and 11143 does not allow for a person or agency to make a request to another person to provide them with a copy of an individual's criminal history or notification that a record does not exist; does not allow an authorized person to furnish the record to an unauthorized person; nor does it allow an unauthorized person to buy, receive or possess the record or information. A violation of these section codes is a misdemeanor.

Sincerely,

Cindy Santos

Record Review Unit
Applicant Information and Certification Program
Bureau of Criminal Information and Analysis

Enclosures
BCIA 8711 (Rev. 06/10)

For KAMALA D. HARRIS
Attorney General

```
4CMTD353332.IH
RE: QHY.CA0349400.29157473.APPUSR.     DATE:20150119 TIME:12:52:38
RESTRICTED-DO NOT USE FOR EMPLOYMENT,LICENSING OR CERTIFICATION PURPOSES
ATTN:APPUSR

** PALM PRINT ON FILE AT DOJ FOR ADDITIONAL INFORMATION PLEASE E-MAIL
PALM.PRINT@DOJ.CA.GOV
** III MULTIPLE SOURCE RECORD
CII/A29157473
DOB/19780110     SEX/M RAC/HISPANIC
HGT/411 WGT/140 EYE/BRO HAI/BLK  POB/PU
CTZ/PERU; UNKNOWN
NAM/001 MEZA,AMERICO ERNESTOAVENI

FBI/553471FC6
SMT/SC L ARM-UNKNOWN
OCC/CONSTRUCION; CONSTRUCTION
* * * *

ARR/DET/CITE:      NAM:001  DOB:19780110
20080320   CASO WOODLAND

CNT:001    #0802235-P00349163
  12500(A) VC-DRIVE W/O LICENSE                      TOC:M
   ARR BY:CAPD DAVIS

CNT:002
  23152(A) VC-DUI ALCOHOL/DRUGS                      TOC:M

CNT:003
  23152(B) VC-DUI ALCOHOL/0.08 PERCENT               TOC:M
   ADR:20080320 (1111,J ST,129, ,DAVIS,CA,95616)
   COM: PHOTO AVAILABLE
   SCN:V35B0800004
* * * *

CUSTODY:JAIL       NAM:001
20110801  CASO WOODLAND

CNT:001    #1104628-P00349163
  -1203.2 PC-PROB VIOL/REARRESTED
  23152(B) VC-DUI ALCOHOL/0.08 PERCENT               TOC:M
   SEN: 005 DAYS WORK FURLOUGH
   ADR:20110801 (4735,COWELL BL,55, ,DAVIS,CA,95618)
   COM: PHOTO AVAILABLE
   COM: CNT 01 NUM-T082178
   SCN:V31E2130001
      *    *    *   END OF MESSAGE   *    *    *
```

TAB 'T':

Docket, Minute and Commitment Sheet (CRM 080002178)

SUPERIOR COURT OF THE STATE OF ...LIFORNIA, COUNTY OF YOLO   DO ...T, MINUTE AND COMMITMENT SHEET

NTA   *3-20 08*

     [REDACTED]   DPT9   5/08/08   CRM 080002178
        8:30AM

ARRAIGNMENT
   001 VC23152(A)   002 VC23152(B)   003 VC12500(A)
   004 VC21658(A)

JUDGE   BERONIO, JANENE CT RPTR   BOOKING FEE $154.48 CLERK *Steven*

APPEARANCES:
- ☑ Deft. appears ☐ In custody ☐ Deft. not appearing
- ☑ With / by Atty. / Pub. Def. *POSTER*
- ☐ Deputy Dist. Atty.
- ☐ Deputy Probation Officer
- ☑ Interpreter sworn *Watkins / Spanish*
- ☐
- ☐ Stip. to Pro-Tem Judge

ARRAIGNMENT:
- ☑ Answers true name as charged
- ☐ Waives reading of Compl / Info / Dec
- ☑ Handed copy of Compl / Info / Dec
- ☑ Handed copy of Discovery
- ☑ Defendant Duly Arraigned
- ☐ Waives Formal Arraignment

REFERRALS ORDERED:
- ☐ _____ Referred to: PUBLIC DEFENDER
- ☐ _____ Referred To: PROBATION
- ☐ Pre-Plea ☐ Bail Study ☐ O.R. Report
- ☐ R & S ☐ Diversion ☐ Supplemental
- ☐ Pub. Def. Conflict Filed; Appointed
- ☐ Report to _____ for booking

ORDERED CONTINUED TO:
- Date *6-12-08* Time *9AM* For *PTC* Dept. *9*
- ☐ _____
- ☐ _____
- ☐ _____
- ☐ Copies to DA _____ 6 ☐ Crt Ack _____ Rpt
- ☐ Continued Party Mot. 8 ☐ Continued Court Mot.

MOTIONS / AMENDMENTS / ORDERS:
- ☐ Motion to / for _____
- ☐ Argued & Submitted ☐ Submitted without argument
- ☐ Granted ☐ Denied ☐ Taken Under Submission
- ☐ Grounds: _____
- ☐ Complaint amended on its face to add CT # _____ a violation of section _____
- ☐ Count # _____ Reduced to _____ ☐ 17b
- ☐ Complaint amended on its face to correct count # _____ to a violation of _____
- ☐ Protective Order signed / filed / served in open court / to remain in effect to _____

WAIVERS / PLEAS:
- ☐ Prior convictions _____
  - ☐ Admitted ☐ Denied
- ☐ Defendant waives Constitutional Rights (SEE REVERSE)
- ☐ Constitutional Rights and plea form filed
- ☐ Pleads Guilty, CT # _____
- ☐ Defendant waives time for sentencing
- ☐ Pleads No Contest, CT # _____
- ☐ Court Finds / Cou Stip: Factual Basis
- ☑ Pleads Not Guilty, CT # *All*
- ☐ Cou / Peo States Reason for Plea on the Record
- ☑ Jury Trial Waived / Demanded *30 JC*
- ☐ Diversion granted, count _____ suspended for _____ months.
- ☑ Time for Trial / PX / Waived / NOT Waived / Cont.
- ☐ Defendant requests permission to withdraw NOT GUILTY / GUILTY / NO CONTEST Plea
- ☐ Per Court / DA dismiss, Complaint / CT # _____

WARRANT ORDERS:
- ☐ Bench / Arrest Warrant to issue
- ☐ Ball Set at $ _____
  - ☐ No NTA / OR Release
- ☐ For _____
- ☐ Recalled ☐ Filed ☐ Set Aside
- ☐ Hold Until _____
- ☐ Held Warrant Issued
- ☐ Civil Assessment Ordered $300.00

PROBATION ORDERS: ☐ Formal ☐ Informal ☐ See Probation Order
- ☐ Probation Reinstated / Modified: Original terms in full force and effect except as follows;
- ☐ Sentenced to _____
- ☐ Case transferred to _____ purs. to 1203.9PC
- ☐ Defendant given rights to Revocation Hearing: Admits / Denies allegations.

- ☐ Sent to State Prison, Execution of Sent. Susp.
- ☐ Probation Revoked: Defendant found in violation of probation.
- ☐ Probation terminated _____
- ☐ Diversion terminated: passed / failed
- ☐ Criminal Proceedings Reinstated / Dismissed
- ☐ Probation Extended to _____
- ☐ Proceedings Susp. _____
- ☐ Def Accepts Prob. / Reinstatement

FINE / REFERRAL ORDERS:
- ☐ Fine (inc. P/A) _____   6 ☐ Other _____
- ☐ A/R Fee $35   7 ☐ _____ Mo./Beginning
- ☐ Court Sec. $20
- ☐ NTA Fee $10   8 ☐ Referred to traffic school
- ☐ Rest 1202.4 $110*$220 $ _____ by _____

- ☐ Proof shown dismiss CT # _____
- ☐ Fine / Jail Suspended on CT # _____
- ☐ Pay attorney fee costs ☐ Misd.   ☐ Felony   ☐ Waived
- ☐ Proof of correction on CT # _____ due by _____
- ☐ $10.00 Fix-It Fee on CT # _____ due _____
- ☐ Civil Assmt. owed $300 or reduced to _____
- ☐ Warrant repo & DMV Fees owed   WR $15   DMV $10

BAIL ORDERS:
- ☐ BB / CB forfeited
- ☐ BB / CB forfeiture set aside and reinstated / exonerated
  - ☐ Upon pmt. of $ _____ for re-assumption fee.
- ☐ BB / CB exonerated

JAIL ORDERS:
- ☐ Be imprisoned _____ hrs / days / months / yr. with CTS
- ☐ Plus _____ days in lieu of fine in ☐ Co. Jail ☐ State Prison
- ☐ See Additional Page for State Prison Sent.
- ☐ Credit for Time Served _____ hrs / days / months
- ☐ Sentence to commence _____
- ☐ Serve consecutive / concurrent with _____

REMANDING ORDERS:
- ☐ Remanded to County Jail Bail set $ _____
- ☐ Remanded to Serve Time
- ☑ Ordered Released ☑ On own OR ☐ Conditional
- ☐ To be transported by Prob. Ofcr. / Program Rep.

DEFENDANT STATUS:
- ☐ OR ☐ BB ☐ CB ☐ NTA / LTA Continued ☐ ROP ☑ OTA
- ☐ Search person / property / residence ☐ Test Alcohol / Drugs
- ☐ Attend Counseling / NA / AA _____ x Week
- ☐ Bring proof at next court date ☐ Counseling to be approved by Probation.

I certify the foregoing copy of judgment rendered on the above date by the above named Judge.

CLERK OF THE COURT BY _____ , DEPUTY
TO THE SHERIFF: The foregoing certified copy of Judgment in the above entitled action is your authority for the execution thereof. (PC1213)

CR310-7/07

SUPERIOR COURT OF THE STATE OF CALIFORNIA, COUNTY OF YOLO   DOCKET, MINUTE AND COMMITMENT SHEET

TW   3-20-00 DPP

DPT 9   6/12/08   CRM 080002178
9:00AM

PTC
001 VC23152(A)   002 VC23152(B)   003 VC12500(A)
004 VC21658(A)   TW
JUDGE   BERONIO, JANENE   CT RPTR   BOOKING FEE $154.48 CLERK Schnab

APPEARANCES:
- ☑ Deft. appears ☐ In custody ☐ Deft. not appearing
- ☑ With / by Atty. / Pub. Def. Father
- ☑ Deputy Dist. Atty. Eddy
- ☐ Deputy Probation Officer
- ☑ Interpreter sworn Saludee L: Spanish
- ☐
- ☐ Stip. to Pro-Tem Judge

ARRAIGNMENT:
- ☐ Answers true name as charged
- ☐ Waives reading of Compl / Info / Dec
- ☐ Handed copy of Compl / Info / Dec
- ☐ Handed copy of Discovery
- ☐ Defendant Duly Arraigned
- ☐ Waives Formal Arraignment

REFERRALS ORDERED:
- ☐ Referred to: PUBLIC DEFENDER
- ☐ Referred To: PROBATION
  - ☐ Pre-Plea ☐ Bail Study ☐ O.R. Report
  - ☐ R & S ☐ Diversion ☐ Supplemental
- ☐ Pub. Def. Conflict Filed; Appointed
- ☐ Report to _____ for booking

ORDERED CONTINUED TO:
Date	Time	For	Dept.
☐			
☐			
☐			
☐			

- ☐ Copies to DA _____ 6 ☐ Crt Ack _____ Rpt
- ☐ Continued Party Mot. 8 ☐ Continued Court Mot.

MOTIONS / AMENDMENTS / ORDERS: BA .11
- ☐ Motion to / for _____
- ☐ Argued & Submitted ☐ Submitted without argument
- ☐ Granted ☐ Denied ☐ Taken Under Submission
  - ☐ Grounds: _____
- ☐ Complaint amended on its face to add CT # _____
  a violation of section _____
- ☐ Count # _____ Reduced to _____ ☐ 17b
- ☐ Complaint amended on its face to correct count # _____
  to a violation of _____
- ☐ Protective Order signed / filed / served in open court / to remain
  in effect to _____

WAIVERS / PLEAS:
- ☑ Defendant waives Constitutional Rights
  (SEE REVERSE)
- ☐ Pleads Guilty, CT # _____
- ☐ Pleads No Contest, CT # _____ 2
- ☐ Pleads Not Guilty, CT # _____
- ☐ Jury Trial Waived / Demanded
- ☐ Time for Trial / PX / Waived / NOT Waived / Cont.
- ☐ Defendant requests permission to withdraw
  NOT GUILTY / GUILTY / NO CONTEST Plea

- ☐ Prior convictions _____
  - ☐ Admitted ☐ Denied
- ☑ Constitutional Rights and plea form filed
- ☑ Defendant waives time for sentencing
- ☐ Court Finds / Cou Stip; Factual Basis
- ☐ Cou / Peo States Reason for Plea on the Record
- ☐ Diversion granted, count _____ suspended
  for _____ months
- ☐ Per Court / DA dismiss, Complaint / CT # 1, 3, 4

WARRANT ORDERS:
- ☐ Bench / Arrest Warrant to Issue
- ☐ Bail Set at $ _____
  - ☐ No NTA / OR Release
- ☐ For _____
- ☐ Recalled ☐ Filed ☐ Set Aside
- ☐ Hold Until _____
- ☐ Hold Warrant Issued
- ☐ Civil Assessment Ordered $300.00

PROBATION ORDERS: ☐ Formal ☑ Informal ☑ See Probation Order
- ☐ Probation Reinstated / Modified: Original terms in full force and
  effect except as follows; 36
- ☐ Sentenced to _____
- ☐ Case transferred to _____ purs. to 1203.9PC
- ☐ Defendant given rights to Revocation Hearing: Admits / Denies allegations.

- ☐ Sent to State Prison, Execution of Sent. Susp.
- ☐ Probation Revoked: Defendant found in violation of probation.
- ☐ Probation terminated _____
- ☐ Diversion terminated; passed / failed
- ☐ Criminal Proceedings Reinstated / Dismissed
- ☐ Probation Extended to _____
- ☐ Proceedings Susp.
- ☐ Def Accepts Prob. / Reinstatement

FINE / REFERRAL ORDERS:
☐ Fine	(Inc. P/A)	6 ☐ Other
☐ A/R Fee	$35	7 ☐ ___ Mo./Beginning
☐ Court Sec.	$20	
☐ NTA Fee	$10	8 ☐ Referred to traffic school
☐ Rest 1202.4	$110/$220	$ ___ by ___

- ☐ Proof shown dismiss CT # _____
- ☐ Fine / Jail Suspended on CT # _____
- ☐ Pay attorney fee costs ☐ Misd. ☐ Felony ☐ Waived
- ☐ Proof of correction on CT # _____ due by _____
- ☐ $10.00 Fix-It Fee on CT # _____ due _____
- ☐ Civil Assmt. owed $300 or reduced to _____
- ☐ Warrant repo & DMV Fees owed   WR $15   DMV $10

BAIL ORDERS:
- ☐ BB / CB forfeited
- ☐ BB / CB forfeiture set aside and reinstated / exonerated
  - ☐ Upon pmt. of $ _____ for re-assumption fee.
- ☐ BB / CB exonerated

JAIL ORDERS: 48 HRS
- ☑ Be Imprisoned 48 HRS _____ hrs / days / months / yr. with CTS
- ☐ Plus _____ days in lieu of fine in ☐ Co. Jail ☐ State Prison
- ☐ See Additional Page for State Prison Sent.
- ☑ Credit for Time Served Jail to calculate ___ days / months
- ☑ Sentence to commence 7/24/08 @ 900
- ☐ Serve consecutive / concurrent with _____

REMANDING ORDERS:
- ☐ Remanded to County Jail Bail set $ _____
- ☐ Remanded to Serve Time
- ☐ Ordered Released ☐ On own OR ☐ Conditional
- ☐ To be transported by Prob. Ofcr. / Program Rep.

DEFENDANT STATUS:
- ☐ OR ☐ SB ☐ CB ☐ NTA / LTA Continued ☑ ROP ☐ OTA
- ☐ Search person / property / residence ☐ Test Alcohol / Drugs
- ☐ Attend Counseling / NA / AA _____ x Week
- ☐ Bring proof at next court date. ☐ Counseling to be approved by Probation.

I certify the foregoing copy of judgment rendered on the above date by the above named Judge.

CLERK OF THE COURT BY Schnab _____, DEPUTY
TO THE SHERIFF: The foregoing certified copy of Judgment in the above entitled action is your authority for the execution thereof. (PC1213)

SUPERIOR COURT OF THE STATE OF CALIFORNIA, COUNTY OF YOLO   DOCKET, MINUTE AND COMMITMENT SHEET

EX PARTE
DPT 9
[23152(B)VC]

10-10-2008

CRM 08-2178
3-20-2008
DPD

JUDGE ROOM 111   CT RPTR   BOOKING FEE $154.48 CLERK **M PATTERSON**
M PATTERSON

APPEARANCES: AT COUNTER
- ☒ Deft. appears ☐ In custody ☐ Deft. not appearing
- ☐ With / by Atty. / Pub. Del.
- ☐ Deputy Dist. Atty.
- ☐ Deputy Probation Officer
- ☐ Interpreter sworn_____ L:
- ☐ Stip. to Pro-Tem Judge

ARRAIGNMENT:
- ☐ Answers true name as charged
- ☐ Waives reading of Compl / Info / Dec
- ☐ Handed copy of Compl / Info / Dec
- ☐ Handed copy of Discovery
- ☐ Defendant Duly Arraigned
- ☐ Waives Formal Arraignment

REFERRALS ORDERED:
- ☐ _____ Referred to: PUBLIC DEFENDER
- ☐ _____ Referred To: PROBATION
  - ☐ Pre-Plea ☐ Bail Study ☐ O.R. Report
  - ☐ R & S ☐ Diversion ☐ Supplemental
- ☐ Pub. Def. Conflict Filed; Appointed
- ☐ Report to _____ for booking

ORDERED CONTINUED TO:
Date	Time	For	Dept.
☐			

☐ RE REFERRED TO 3 MONTH ABC PROGRAM

☐ MUST COMPLETE BY 4-12-2009

☐ _____
- ☐ Copies to DA _____ 6 ☐ Crl Ack _____ Rpt
- ☐ Continued Party Mot. 8 ☐ Continued Court Mot.

MOTIONS / AMENDMENTS / ORDERS:
- ☐ Motion to / for _____
- ☐ Argued & Submitted ☐ Submitted without argument
- ☐ Granted ☐ Denied ☐ Taken Under Submission
  - ☐ Grounds: _____
- ☐ Complaint amended on its face to add CT # _____ a violation of section _____
- ☐ Count # _____ Reduced to _____ ☐ 17b
- ☐ Complaint amended on its face to correct count # _____ to a violation of _____
- ☐ Protective Order signed / filed / served in open court / to remain in effect to _____

WAIVERS / PLEAS:
- ☐ Defendant waives Constitutional Rights (SEE REVERSE)
- ☐ Pleads Guilty, CT #
- ☐ Pleads No Contest, CT #
- ☐ Pleads Not Guilty, CT #
- ☐ Jury Trial Waived / Demanded
- ☐ Time for Trial / PX / Waived / NOT Waived / Cont.
- ☐ Defendant requests permission to withdraw NOT GUILTY / GUILTY / NO CONTEST Plea

☐ Prior convictions
   ☐ Admitted ☐ Denied
- ☐ Constitutional Rights and plea form filed
- ☐ Defendant waives time for sentencing
- ☐ Court Finds / Cou Stip; Factual Basis
- ☐ Cou / Peo States Reason for Plea on the Record
- ☐ Diversion granted, count _____ suspended for _____ months.
- ☐ Per Court / DA dismiss, Complaint / CT # ____

WARRANT ORDERS:
- ☐ Bench / Arrest Warrant to issue
- ☐ Bail Set at $
  - ☐ No NTA / OR Release
- ☐ For
- ☐ Recalled ☐ Filed ☐ Set Aside
- ☐ Hold Until
- ☐ Held Warrant Issued
- ☐ Civil Assessment Ordered $300.00

PROBATION ORDERS: ☐ Formal ☐ Informal ☐ See Probation Order
- ☐ Probation Reinstated / Modified: Original terms in full force and effect except as follows;
- ☐ Sentenced to _____
- ☐ Case transferred to _____ purs. to 1203.9PC
- ☐ Defendant given rights to Revocation Hearing: Admits / Denies allegations.

- ☐ Sent to State Prison, Execution of Sent. Susp.
- ☐ Probation Revoked: Defendant found in violation of probation.
- ☐ Probation terminated
- ☐ Diversion terminated: passed / failed
- ☐ Criminal Proceedings Reinstated / Dismissed
- ☐ Probation Extended to
- ☐ Proceedings Susp.
- ☐ Def Accepts Prob. / Reinstatement

FINE / REFERRAL ORDERS:
☐ Fine	(Inc. P/A)	6 ☐ Other	
☐ A/R Fee	$35	7 ☐ ___ Mo./Beginning	
☐ Court Sec.	$20		
☐ NTA Fee	$10	8 ☐ Referred to traffic school	
☐ Rest 1202.4	$110/$220	$ ___ by ___	

- ☐ Proof shown dismiss CT #
- ☐ Fine / Jail Suspended on CT #
- ☐ Pay attorney fee costs ☐ Misd. ☐ Felony ☐ Waived
- ☐ Proof of correction on CT # _____ due by _____
- ☐ $10.00 Fix-It Fee on CT # _____ due _____
- ☐ Civil Assmt. owed $300 or reduced to _____
- ☐ Warrant repo & DMV Fees owed   WR $15   DMV $10

BAIL ORDERS:
- ☐ BB / CB forfeited
- ☐ BB / CB forfeiture set aside and reinstated / exonerated
  - ☐ Upon pmt. of $_____ for re-assumption fee.
- ☐ BB / CB exonerated

JAIL ORDERS:
- ☐ Be imprisoned _____ hrs / days / months / yr. with CTS
  - ☐ Plus _____ days in lieu of fine in ☐ Co. Jail ☐ State Prison
  - ☐ See Additional Page for State Prison Sent.
- ☐ Credit for Time Served _____ hrs / days / months
- ☐ Sentence to commence _____
- ☐ Serve consecutive / concurrent with _____

REMANDING ORDERS:
- ☐ Remanded to County Jail Bail set $
- ☐ Remanded to Serve Time
- ☐ Ordered Released ☐ On own OR ☐ Conditional
- ☐ To be transported by Prob. Ofcr. / Program Rep.

DEFENDANT STATUS:
- ☐ OR ☐ BB ☐ CB ☐ NTA / LTA Continued ☐ ROP ☐ OTA
- ☐ Search person / property / residence ☐ Test Alcohol / Drugs
- ☐ Attend Counseling / NA / AA _____ x Week
- ☐ Bring proof at next court date. ☐ Counseling to be approved by Probation.

I certify the foregoing copy of judgment rendered on the above date by the above named Judge.

CLERK OF THE COURT BY _____ DEPUTY   CC D.A.

TO THE SHERIFF: The foregoing certified copy of Judgment in the above entitled action is your authority for the execution thereof. (PC1213)

CR370-7/07

TAB 'J':

Docket, Minute and Commitment (CRM 110001336)

SUPERIOR COURT OF THE STATE OF CALIFORNIA, COUNTY OF YOLO   DOCKET, MINUTE AND COMMITMENT SHEET

DPT9   3/28/11   CRM 110001336
                                       8:30AM

ARRAIGNMENT
001 VC14601.5(A)   002 VC21461(A)
                    Warnier
JUDGE BERONIO, JANENE D.   CT RPTR _____   BOOKING FEE $154.48 CLERK Medes

APPEARANCES:
- Def't appears ☐ In custody ☐ Def't not appearing
- With / by Atty. / Pub. Def. _____ Roos
- Deputy Dist. Atty. _____ (916) 923-2361
- Deputy Probation Officer _____
- Interpreter sworn _____ L: _____
- ☐
- Stip. to Pro-Tem Judge

ARRAIGNMENT:
- ☑ Answers true name as charged
- ☐ _____
- ☑ Waives reading of Compl / Info / Dec
- ☑ Handed copy of Compl / Info / Dec
- ☑ Handed copy of Discovery
- ☑ Defendant Duly Arraigned
- ☑ Waives Formal Arraignment

REFERRALS ORDERED:
- ☐ _____ Referred to: PUBLIC DEFENDER
- ☐ _____ Referred to: PROBATION
  - ☐ Pre-Plea ☐ Bail Study ☐ O.R. Report
  - ☐ R & S ☐ Diversion ☐ Supplemental
- ☐ Pub. Def. Conflict Filed; Appointed
- ☐ _____
- ☐ Report to _____ for booking

ORDERED CONTINUED TO:

Date	Time	For	Dept
☑ 5-10-1	10:20	PTC	9
☐			
☐			
☐			

- ☐ Copies to DA _____ 6 ☐ Crt Ack _____ Rpt
- ☐ Cont Party's / Court's Motion 8 ☐ LDFM: _____

MOTIONS / AMENDMENTS / ORDERS:
- ☐ Motion to / for _____
- ☑ Argued & Submitted ☐ Submitted without argument
- ☑ Granted ☐ Denied ☐ Taken Under Submission
  - ☐ Grounds: _____
- ☐ Complaint amended on its face to add CT # _____
  a violation of section _____
- ☐ Count # _____ Reduced to _____ ☐ 17b
- ☐ Complaint amended on its face to correct count # _____
  to a violation of _____
- ☐ Protective Order signed / filed / served in open court / to remain
  in effect to _____

WAIVERS / PLEAS:
- ☐ Def't waives Constitutional Rights
- ☐ Pleads Guilty, CT # _____
- ☐ Pleads No Contest, CT # _____
- ☑ Pleads Not Guilty, CT # 1-2
- ☑ Jury Trial Waived / Demanded
- ☐ Time for Trial ☐ PX ☑ Wvd ☐ Not Wvd ☐ Cont.
- ☐ Def't req's permission to w/d Plea of _____

- ☐ Prior Conv. / ENH _____
  - ☐ Admitted ☐ Denied
- ☐ Constitutional Rights and Plea Form Filed
- ☐ Defendant waives time for sentencing
- ☐ Court Finds / Cou Stip: Factual Basis
- ☐ Cou / Peo State Reason for Plea on Record
- ☐ DIV granted, CT# _____ susp'd for _____ mos.
- ☐ Per Court/DA dismiss Complaint/CT#

WARRANT ORDERS:
- ☐ Bench / Arrest Warrant to Issue
  - Bail Set at $ _____
  - ☐ No NTA / OR Release ☐ NTS
  - ☐ For _____
- ☐ Recalled ☐ Filed ☐ Set Aside
- ☐ Hold Until _____
- ☐ Held Warrant Issued
- ☐ Civil Assessment Ordered $300.00

PROBATION ORDERS: ☐ Formal ☐ Informal ☐ See Probation Order
- ☐ Probation Reinstated / Modified; Original terms in full force and
  effect except as follows;
- ☐ Sentenced to _____
- ☐ Case transferred to _____ purs. to 1203.9PC
- ☐ Defendant given rights to Revocation Hearing; Admits / Denies allegations.

- ☐ Sent to State Prison, Execution of Sent. Susp.
- ☐ Probation Revoked; Defendant found in violation of probation.
- ☐ Probation terminated _____
- ☐ Diversion terminated; passed / failed
- ☐ Criminal Proceedings Reinstated / Dismissed
- ☐ Probation Extended to _____
- ☐ Proceedings Susp _____
- ☐ Def Accepts Prob. / Reinstatement

FINE / REFERRAL ORDERS: Fine (Inc P/A) $ _____ PLUS
- SEC FEE $ _____ CCA FEE $ _____ ☐ NTA FEE $10.00
- ☐ A/R FEE $35.00 ☐ REST 1202.4 $110/$220 ☐ Other: _____
- ☐ DUE _____ ☐ PMTS $ _____ PER MO BEG _____
- REF TO TRAFFIC SCHOOL $ _____ BY _____

- ☐ POC shown Dism CT# _____ Fee $ _____ Due _____
- ☐ POC on CT# _____ Due _____
- ☐ Fine / Jail Susp on CT# _____
- ☐ Pay Atty Fees ☐ Misd ☐ Felony ☐ Waived
- ☐ Civil Assmt Owed ☐ $300 ☐ Reduced to $ _____ ☐ + Fees

BAIL ORDERS:
- ☐ BB / CB / PB forfeited
- ☐ BB / CB / PB forfeiture set aside and reinstated / exonerated
  - ☐ Upon pml. of $ _____ for re-assumption fee.
- ☐ BB / CB / PB exonerated
- ☐ SDT Released to: _____

JAIL ORDERS:
- ☐ Be imprisoned _____ hrs / days / months / yr. with CTS
- ☐ Plus _____ days in lieu of fine in ☐ Co. Jail ☐ State Prison
- ☐ See Additional Page for State Prison Sent.
- ☐ Credit for Time Served _____ hrs / days / months
- ☐ Sentence to commence _____
- ☐ Serve consecutive / concurrent with _____

REMANDING ORDERS:
- ☐ Remanded to County Jail Bail set $ _____
- ☐ Remanded to Serve Time
- ☐ Ordered Released ☐ On own OR ☐ Conditional
- ☐ To be transported by Prob. Ofcr. / Program Rep.

DEFENDANT STATUS:
- OR ☐ BB ☐ CB ☐ PB ☐ NR / UA Continued ☐ RCP ☐ OR
- ☐ Search person / property / residence ☐ Test Alcohol / Drugs
- ☐ Attend Counseling / NA / AA _____ x Week
- ☐ Bring proof at next court date. ☐ Counseling to be approved by Probation.

I certify the foregoing copy of judgment rendered on the above date by the above named Judge.

CLERK OF THE COURT BY _____ , DEPUTY
TO THE SHERIFF: The foregoing certified copy of Judgment in the above entitled action is your authority for the execution thereof. (PC1213)

CR370-06/10

SUPERIOR COURT OF THE STATE OF CALIFORNIA, COUNTY OF YOLO   DOCKET, MINUTE AND COMMITMENT SHEET

AVENIO   DPT9   5/10/11   CRM 110001336
AMERICO MEZA   10:30AM
PTC
    001 VC14601.5(A)   C02 VC21461(A)

JUDGE BERONIO, JANENE D   CT RPTR_____   BOOKING FEE $154.48 CLERK _____

APPEARANCES:
- [ ] Deft. appears [ ] In custody [ ] Deft. not appearing
- [ ] With Key Atty [ ] Pub. Def. _____
- [ ] Deputy Dist. Atty. _____
- [ ] Deputy Probation Officer _____
- [ ] Interpreter sworn _____ L: _____
- [ ] Stip. to Pro-Tem Judge

ARRAIGNMENT:
- [ ] Answers true name as charged
- [ ] Waives reading of Compl / Info / Dec
- [ ] Handed copy of Compl / Info / Dec
- [ ] Handed copy of Discovery
- [ ] Defendant Duly Arraigned
- [ ] Waives Formal Arraignment

REFERRALS ORDERED:
- [ ] _____ Referred to: PUBLIC DEFENDER
- [ ] _____ Referred to: PROBATION
- [ ] Pre-Plea [ ] Bail Study [ ] O.R. Report
- [ ] R & S [ ] Diversion [ ] Supplemental
- [ ] Pub. Def. Conflict Filed; Appointed
- [ ] Report to _____ for booking

ORDERED CONTINUED TO:
- [ ] Date 6/14/11 Time 10:30 For PTC _____
- [ ] _____
- [ ] _____
- [ ] _____
- [ ] Copies to DA _____ 6 [ ] Crt Ack _____ Rpt
- [ ] Cont Party's / Court's Motion 8 [ ] LDFM: _____

MOTIONS / AMENDMENTS / ORDERS:
- [ ] Motion to / for _____
- [ ] Argued & Submitted [ ] Submitted without argument
- [ ] Granted [ ] Denied [ ] Taken Under Submission
  - [ ] Grounds: _____
- [ ] Complaint amended on its face to add CT # _____
  - a violation of section _____
- [ ] Count # _____ Reduced to _____ [ ] 17b
- [ ] Complaint amended on its face to correct count # _____
  - to a violation of _____
- [ ] Protective Order signed / filed / served in open court / to remain
  - in effect to _____

WAIVERS / PLEAS:
- [ ] Deft waives Constitutional Rights
- [ ] Pleads Guilty, CT # _____
- [ ] Pleads No Contest, CT # _____
- [ ] Pleads Not Guilty, CT # _____
- [ ] Jury Trial Waived / Demanded
- [ ] Time for Trial [ ] PX [ ] Wvd [ ] Not Wvd [ ] Cont.
- [ ] Deft req's permission to w/d Plea of _____

- [ ] Prior Conv. / ENH _____
  - [ ] Admitted [ ] Denied
- [ ] Constitutional Rights and Plea Form Filed
- [ ] Defendant waives time for sentencing
- [ ] Court Finds / Cou Stips Factual Basis
- [ ] Cou / Peo State Reason for Plea on Record
- [ ] DIV granted, CT# _____ susp'd for _____ mos.
- [ ] Per Court/DA dismiss Complaint/CT# _____

WARRANT ORDERS:
- [ ] Bench / Arrest Warrant to Issue
  - Bail Set at $ _____
  - [ ] No NTA / OR Release [ ] NTS
- [ ] For _____
- [ ] Recalled [ ] Filed [ ] Set Aside
- [ ] Hold Until _____
- [ ] Held Warrant Issued
- [ ] Civil Assessment Ordered $300.00

PROBATION ORDERS: [ ] Formal [ ] Informal [ ] See Probation Order
- [ ] Probation Reinstated / Modified: Original terms in full force and effect except as follows;
- [ ] Sentenced to _____
- [ ] Case transferred to _____ purs. to 1203.9PC
- [ ] Defendant given rights to Revocation Hearing: Admits / Denies allegations.

- [ ] Sent to State Prison, Execution of Sent. Susp.
- [ ] Probation Revoked; Defendant found in violation of probation.
- [ ] Probation terminated _____
- [ ] Diversion terminated: passed / failed
- [ ] Criminal Proceedings Reinstated / Dismissed
- [ ] Probation Extended to _____
- [ ] Proceedings Susp _____
- [ ] Def Accepts Prob. / Reinstatement

FINE / REFERRAL ORDERS: Fine (Inc P/A) $ _____ PLUS
- SEC FEE $ _____ CCA FEE $ _____ [ ] NTA FEE $10.00
- [ ] A/R FEE $35.00 [ ] REST 1202.4 $110/$220 [ ] Other: _____
- [ ] DUE _____ [ ] PMTS $ _____ PER MO BEG _____
- REF TO TRAFFIC SCHOOL $ _____ BY _____

- [ ] POC shown Dism CT# _____ Fee $ _____ Due _____
- [ ] POC on CT# _____ Due _____
- [ ] Fine / Jail Susp on CT# _____
- [ ] Pay Atty Fees [ ] Misd [ ] Felony [ ] Waived
- [ ] Civil Assmt Owed [ ] $300 [ ] Reduced to $ _____ [ ] + Fees

BAIL ORDERS:
- [ ] BB / CB / PB forfeited
- [ ] BB / CB / PB forfeiture set aside and reinstated / exonerated
  - [ ] Upon pmt. of $ _____ for re-assumption fee.
- [ ] BB / CB / PB exonerated
- [ ] SDT Released to: _____

JAIL ORDERS:
- [ ] Be imprisoned _____ hrs / days / months / yr. with CTS
  - [ ] Plus _____ days in lieu of fine in [ ] Co. Jail [ ] State Prison
  - [ ] See Additional Page for State Prison Sent.
- [ ] Credit for Time Served _____ hrs / days / months
- [ ] Sentence to commence _____
- [ ] Serve consecutive / concurrent with _____

REMANDING ORDERS:
- [ ] Remanded to County Jail Bail set $ _____
- [ ] Remanded to Serve Time
- [ ] Ordered Released [ ] On own OR [ ] Conditional
- [ ] To be transported by Prob. Ofcr. / Program Rep.

DEFENDANT STATUS:
- [ ] OR [ ] BB [ ] CB [ ] PB [x] NTA / LTA Continued [ ] ROP [x] OTA
- [ ] Search person / property / residence [ ] Test Alcohol / Drugs
- [ ] Attend Counseling / NA / AA _____ x Week
- [ ] Bring proof at next court date. [ ] Counseling to be approved by Probation

I certify the foregoing copy of judgment rendered upon the above date by the above named Judge.

CLERK OF THE COURT BY _____ , DEPUTY
TO THE SHERIFF: The foregoing certified copy of Judgment in the above entitled action is your authority for the execution thereof. (PC1213)

CR370-05/10

DPT9   6/14/11   CRM 110001336
10:30AM

P1C
NTA 001-VC14601.51A7   002 VC21461(A)   3)VC 14601.1 (a)

JUDGE BERONIO, JANENE D CT RPTR   BOOKING FEE $164.48 CLERK Ingraham

APPEARANCES:
☐ Deft. appears ☐ In custody ☒ Deft. not appearing
☒ With Atty ☐ Pub. Def. FOOS
☒ Deputy Dist. Atty. Hasaper
☐ Deputy Probation Officer
☐ Interpreter sworn _____ L: _____
☐ Stip. to Pro-Tem Judge

ARRAIGNMENT:
☐ Answers true name as charged
☐ Waives reading of Compl / Info / Dec
☐ Handed copy of Compl / Info / Dec
☐ Handed copy of Discovery
☐ Defendant Duly Arraigned
☐ Waives Formal Arraignment

REFERRALS ORDERED:
☐ _____ Referred to: PUBLIC DEFENDER
☐ _____ Referred to: PROBATION
☐ Pre-Plea ☐ Bail Study ☐ O.R. Report
☐ R & S ☐ Diversion ☐ Supplemental
☐ Pub. Def. Conflict Filed; Appointed
☐ Report to _____ for booking

ORDERED CONTINUED TO:
Date	Time	For signed	Dept.
6-28-11	1:30	P.O.	9

☐ Copies to DA _____ 6 ☐ Crt Ack _____ Rpt
☐ Cont Party's / Court's Motion 8 ☐ LDFM:

MOTIONS / AMENDMENTS / ORDERS:
☐ Motion to / for _____
☐ Argued & Submitted ☐ Submitted without argument
☐ Granted ☐ Denied ☐ Taken Under Submission
☐ Grounds: _____
☒ Complaint amended on its face to add CT # 3
a violation of section VC 14601.1 (a)
☐ Count # _____ Reduced to _____ ☐ 17b
☐ Complaint amended on its face to correct count #
to a violation of _____
☐ Protective Order signed / filed / served in open court / to remain
in effect to _____

WAIVERS / PLEAS:
☒ Def't waives Constitutional Rights
☐ Pleads Guilty, CT # _____
☒ Pleads No Contest, CT # 3
☐ Pleads Not Guilty, CT #
☐ Jury Trial Waived / Demanded
☐ Time for Trial ☐ PX ☐ Wvd ☐ Not Wvd ☐ Cont.
☐ Def't req's permission to w/d Plea of _____

☐ Prior Conv. / ENH
☐ Admitted ☐ Denied
☒ Constitutional Rights and Plea Form Filed
☒ Defendant waives time for sentencing
☐ Court Finds / Cou Stip: Factual Basis
☐ Cou / Peo State Reason for Plea on Record
☐ DIV granted, CT# _____ susp'd for _____ mos.
☒ Per Court Dismiss Complaint CT#
1 & 2

WARRANT ORDERS:
☐ Bench / Arrest Warrant to Issue
Bail Set at $ _____
☐ No NTA / OR Release ☐ NTS
☐ For _____
☐ Recalled ☐ Filed ☐ Set Aside
☐ Hold Until _____
☐ Hold Warrant Issued
☐ Civil Assessment Ordered $300.00

PROBATION ORDERS: ☐ Formal ☒ Informal ☒ See Probation Order
☐ Probation Reinstated / Modified: Original terms in full force and 12 mo
effect except as follows;
☐ Sentenced to _____

☐ Case transferred to _____ purs. to 1203.9PC
☐ Defendant given rights to Revocation Hearing; Admits / Denies allegations.

☐ Sent to State Prison, Execution of Sent. Susp.
☐ Probation Revoked: Defendant found in violation of probation.
☐ Probation terminated _____
☐ Diversion terminated: passed / failed
☐ Criminal Proceedings Reinstated / Dismissed
☐ Probation Extended to _____
☐ Proceedings Susp _____
☒ Def Accepts Prob. / Reinstatement

FINE / REFERRAL ORDERS: Fine (Inc P/A) $ 1404 00 PLUS
or $1404.00 w/PAC
SEC FEE $ ____ CCA FEE $ ____ ☐ NTA FEE $10.00
☒ A/R FEE $35.00 ☐ REST 1202.4 $110/$220 ☐ Other: _____
☐ DUE ____ PMTS $ 100 / PER MO BEG 7-14-11
REF TO TRAFFIC SCHOOL $ _____ BY _____

☐ POC shown Dism CT# _____ Fee $ _____ Due _____
☒ POC on CT# 3 Due 8-15-11 Susp. $1500.00
☐ Fine / Jail Susp on CT# _____
☐ Pay Atty Fees ☐ Misd ☐ Felony ☐ Waived
☐ Civil Asstmt Owed ☐ $300 ☐ Reduced to $ _____ ☐ + Fees

BAIL ORDERS:
☐ BB / CB / PB forfeited
☐ BB / CB / PB forfeiture set aside and reinstated / exonerated
☐ Upon pmt. of $ _____ for re-assumption fee.
☐ BB / CB / PB exonerated
☐ SDT Released to: _____

JAIL ORDERS:
☐ Be imprisoned _____ hrs / days / months / yr. with CTS
☐ Plus _____ days in lieu of fine in ☐ Co. Jail ☐ State Prison
☐ See Additional Page for State Prison Sent.
☐ Credit for Time Served _____ hrs / days / months
☐ Sentence to commence _____
☐ Serve consecutive / concurrent with _____

REMANDING ORDERS:
☐ Remanded to County Jail Bail set $ _____
☐ Remanded to Serve Time
☐ Ordered Released ☐ On own OR ☐ Conditional
☐ To be transported by Prob. Ofcr. / Program Rep.

DEFENDANT STATUS:
☐ OR ☐ BB ☐ CB ☐ PB ☐ NTA / LTA Continued ☒ ROP ☐ OTA
☐ Search person / property / residence ☐ Test Alcohol / Drugs
☐ Attend Counseling / NA / AA _____ x Week
☐ Bring proof at next court date. ☐ Counseling to be approved by Probation.

I certify the foregoing copy of judgment rendered on the above date by the above named Judge.
CLERK OF THE COURT BY _____ , DEPUTY
TO THE SHERIFF: The foregoing certified copy of judgment in the above entitled action is your authority for the execution thereof. (PC1213) CR170-06/10

TAB 'K':

NTA and DHS Request to Reschedule NTA Interactive Scheduling System

In removal proceedings under section 240 of the Immigration and Nationality Act

File No: A098 350 736
Case No: FLF0510000363
FIN #: 16026916

In the Matter of:

Respondent: ████████████████████████████ ████████████████████ _____ currently residing at:

████████████
(Number, street, city state and ZIP code)   (Area code and phone number)

☐ 1. You are an arriving alien.

☒ 2. You are an alien present in the United States who has not been admitted or paroled.

☐ 3. You have been admitted to the United States, but are deportable for the reasons stated below.

The Service alleges that you:

See Continuation Page Made a Part Hereof

On the basis of the foregoing, it is charged that you are subject to removal from the United States pursuant to the following provision(s) of law:

See Continuation Page Made a Part Hereof

☐ This notice is being issued after an asylum officer has found that the respondent has demonstrated a credible fear of persecution or torture.

☐ Section 235(b)(1) order was vacated pursuant to: ☐ 8 CFR 208.30(f)(2) ☐ 8 CFR 235.3(b)(5)(iv)

YOU ARE ORDERED to appear before an immigration judge of the United States Department of Justice at: _____
606 S. Olive Street Suite 1500 Los Angeles CALIFORNIA US 90014
(Complete Address of Immigration Court, Including Room Number, if any)

On November 19, 2004   at 01:00 p.m. _____ to show why you should not be removed from the United States based on the
     (Date)   (Time)
charge(s) set forth above.

THOMAS SLOWINSKI
SUPERVISORY BORDER PATROL AGENT
(Signature and Title of Issuing Officer)

Date: October 19, 2004   Falfurrias, Texas
                                          (City and State)

See reverse for important information

Notice to Respondent

Warning: Any statement you make may be used against you in removal proceedings.

Alien Registration: This copy of the Notice to Appear served upon you is evidence of your alien registration while you are under removal proceedings. You are required to carry it with you at all times.

Representation: If you so choose, you may be represented in this proceeding, at no expense to the Government, by an attorney or other individual authorized and qualified to represent persons before the Executive Office for Immigration Review, pursuant to 8 CFR 3.16. Unless you so request, no hearing will be scheduled earlier than ten days from the date of this notice to allow you sufficient time to secure counsel. A list of qualified attorneys and organizations who may be available to represent you at no cost will be provided with this Notice.

Conduct of the hearing: At the time of your hearing, you should bring with you any affidavits or other documents which you desire to have considered in connection with your case. If any document is in a foreign language, you must bring the original and a certified English translation of the document. If you wish to have the testimony of any witnesses considered, you should arrange to have such witnesses present at the hearing.

At your hearing you will be given the opportunity to admit or deny any or all of the allegations in the Notice to Appear and that you are inadmissible or deportable on the charges contained in the Notice to Appear. You will have an opportunity to present evidence on your own behalf, to examine any evidence presented by the Government, to object, on proper legal grounds, to the receipt of evidence and to cross examine any witnesses presented by the Government. At the conclusion of your hearing, you have a right to appeal an adverse decision by the immigration judge.

You will be advised by the immigration judge before whom you appear, of any relief from removal for which you may appear eligible including the privilege of departing voluntarily. You will be given a reasonable opportunity to make any such application to the immigration judge.

Failure to appear: You are required to provide the INS, in writing, with your full mailing address and telephone number. You must notify the Immigration Court immediately by using Form EOIR-33 whenever you change your address or telephone number during the course of this proceeding. You will be provided with a copy of this form. Notices of hearing will be mailed to this address. If you do not submit Form EOIR-33 and do not otherwise provide an address at which you may be reached during proceedings, then the Government shall not be required to provide you with written notice of your hearing. If you fail to attend the hearing at the time and place designated on this notice, or any date and time later directed by the Immigration Court, a removal order may be made by the immigration judge in your absence, and you may be arrested and detained by the INS.

Request for Prompt Hearing

To expedite a determination in my case, I request an immediate hearing. I waive my right to have a 10-day period prior to appearing before an immigration judge.

Before: _____

_____
(Signature of Respondent)

_____
(Signature and Title of INS Officer)

Date: _____

Certificate of Service

This Notice to Appear was served on the respondent by me on **October 19, 2004**, in the following manner and in
(Date)
compliance with section 239(a)(1)(F) of the Act:

☒ in person ☐ by certified mail, return receipt requested ☐ by regular mail
☐ Attached is a credible fear worksheet.
☒ Attached is a list of organizations and attorneys which provide free legal services.
The alien was provided oral notice in the **SPANISH** _____ language of the time and place of his or her hearing and of the consequences of failure to appear as provided in section 240(b)(7) of the Act.

_____
(Signature of Respondent if Personally Served)

RODOLFO MORENO
BORDER PATROL AGENT
_____
(Signature and Title of Officer)

Form I-862 (Rev. 1/31/2001)

U.S. Department of Justice
Immigration and Naturalization Service

Continuation Page for Form   I-862

Alien's Name	File Number	Date
[redacted]	Case No: FLF0510000363 A[redacted]	October 19, 2004

The Service alleges that you:

1) You are not a citizen or national of the United States;

2) You are a native of PERU and a citizen of PERU;

3) You arrived in the United States at or near HIDALGO, TEXAS, on or about October 15, 2004;

4) You were not then admitted or paroled after inspection by an Immigration Officer.

On the basis of the foregoing, it is charged that you are subject to removal from the United States pursuant to the following provision(s) of law:

212(a)(6)(A)(i) of the Immigration and Nationality Act, as amended, in that you are an alien present in the United States without being admitted or paroled, or who arrived in the United States at any time or place other than as designated by the Attorney General.

Signature	Title
THOMAS SLOWINSKI	SUPERVISORY BORDER PATROL AGENT

 3 of 3 Pages

Form I-831 Continuation Page (Rev. 6/12/92)

Request to Reschedule NTA
Interactive Scheduling System

File Number: A▮▮▮▮▮   Date: June 20, 2008

Alien's Name, Address, and City/State/Zip:

▮▮▮▮▮▮▮▮▮▮

Date NTA Submitted: June 23, 2008
(*cannot be earlier than date of hearing below*)

This case was scheduled to be heard on November 19, 2004, at 1:00 p.m., through the pilot project, however, the Notice to Appear (NTA) was not timely filed with the Office of the Immigration Judge.

It is being submitted for a new hearing date pursuant to the guidelines of the pilot project. An original NTA is attached.

I certify that a copy of the foregoing was served on the above respondent/applicant **by mail** to the above address on 6/23/08.

Kristin Piepmeier
Assistant Chief Counsel
U.S. Department of Homeland Security
Los Angeles, California

TAB 'L':

Record of Deportable/Inadmissible Alien

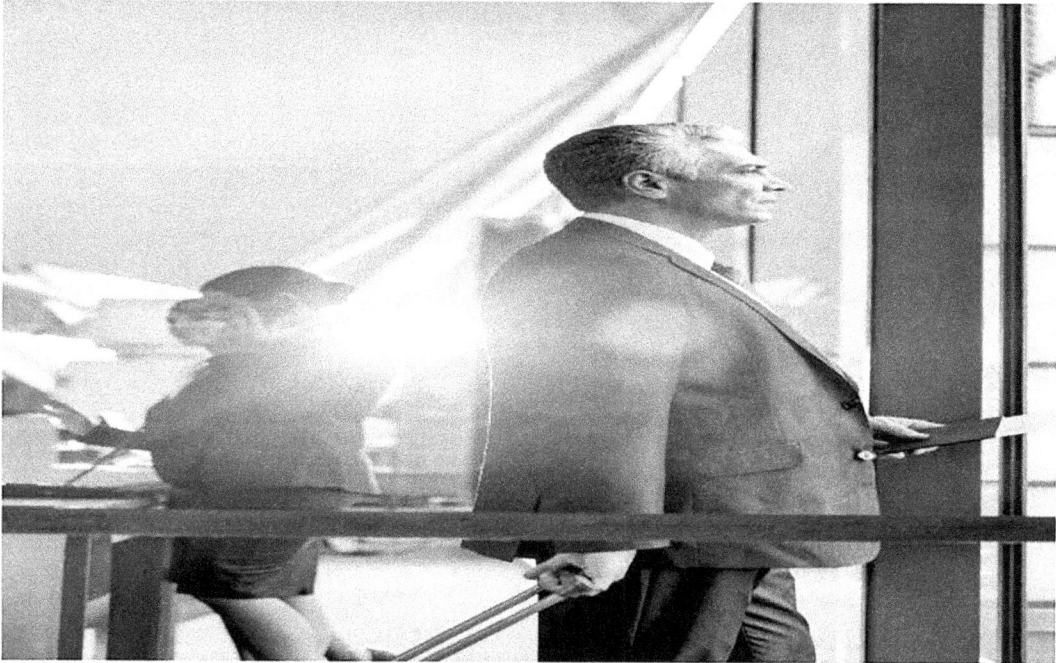

Record of Deportable/Inadmissible Alien

Family Name (CAPS)	First	Middle	Sex M	Hair BLK	Eyes BRO	Cmplxn MED
Country of Citizenship PERU	Passport Number and Country of Issue	Case No: FLF0510000363 File Number A098 350 736	Height 67	Weight 155	Occupation LABORER	

U.S. Address
1110 NANTUCKET TER
DAVIS, CALIFORNIA 95616

Date, Place, Time, and Manner of Last Entry 10/15/2004, 1247, HID, FWA, Wade	Passenger Boarded at	Scars and Marks See Narrative	

Number, Street, City, Province (State) and Country of Permanent Residence URBANIZACION LAS GARDENIAS DE GLORIA MANZANA A LOTE 17 CONCEPCION, DEPT. JUNIN PERU	F.B.I. Number 553471FC6	☒ Single ☐ Divorced ☐ Married ☐ Widower ☐ Separated

Date of Birth 01/10/1978 Age: 26	Date of Action 10/19/2004	Location Code MCA/FLF	Method of Location/Apprehension PI 518.3

City, Province (State) and Country of Birth CONCEPCION, DEPT. JUNIN, PERU	AR ☒	Forms (Type and No.)	Lifted ☐	Not Lifted ☐	At/Near FALFURRIAS, TEXAS	Date/Hour 10/19/2004 1247

NIV Issuing Post and NIV Number	Social Security Account Name	By See Narrative	Status at Entry FWA Mexico	Status When Found TRAVEL/SEEKING

Date Visa Issued	Social Security Number	Length of Time Illegally in U.S. AT ENTRY

Immigration Record NEGATIVE - See Narrative	Criminal Record None known	

Name, Address, and Nationality of Spouse (Maiden Name, if Appropriate)	Number and Nationality of Minor Children NONE

Father's Name, Nationality, and Address, if Known Nationality: PERU MENA-QUINTANA, Guillermo SFA	Mother's Present and Maiden Names, Nationality, and Address, if Known AVENIO-VASQUEZ, Epifania SFA

Monies Due/Property in U.S. Not in Immediate Possession	Fingerprinted? Yes ☒ No ☐	INS Systems Checks See Narrative	Charge Code Word(s) 16A

Name and Address of (Last)/(Current) U.S. Employer	Type of Employment	Salary Hr / /	Employed from/to / /

Narrative (Outline particulars under which alien was located/apprehended. Include details not shown above regarding time, place and manner of last entry, attempted entry, or any other entry, and elements which establish administrative and/or criminal violation. Indicate means and route of travel to interior.)

FIN #: 16026916

SCARS, MARKS AND TATTOOS
None Visible

APPREHENDED BY
GABRIEL SALAZAR
SERGIO H. RAMIREZ

MOTHER'S NATIONALITY
PERU

FUNDS IN POSSESSION
87.00   United States Dollar

INS SYSTEMS CHECKS
Central Index System Negative
Deportable Alien Control System Negative
Integrated Automated Fingerprint Identification System Negative
Interagency Border Inspection System Negative
National Automated Immigration Lookout System Negative
National Crime Information Center Negative
Non Immigrant Information System Negative

Alien has been advised of communication privileges. 10/19/04 (Date/Initials)	RODOLFO MORENO BORDER PATROL AGENT (Signature and Title of INS Official)

Distribution: A: FILE G-23 FLF	Received: (Subject and Documents) (Report of Interview) Officer: RODOLFO MORENO on: October 19, 2004 at 1258 (time) Disposition: Warrant of Arrest/Notice to Appear Examining Officer: CARLOS R. TREVINO

Alien's Name	File Number	Date
███████████████	Case No: FLF0510000363	10/19/2004

Treasury Enforcement Communications System Negative

Narrative Title: Record of Deportable/Excludable Alien
Narrative Created by PENA III

IMMIGRATION DATA: Subject is a citizen and national of Peru by birth. Subject is not in possession of any immigration documents nor are there any petitions pending on his behalf in order to remain in the United States legally.

ENTRY DATA: Subject stated that he entered the United States by wading across the Rio Grande River near the Hidalgo, Texas Port of Entry on October 15, 2004. Subject entered the United States at a place not designated as a Port of Entry by the Attorney General of the United States and or the Secretary of Homeland Security, the successor, thus he was not admitted, inspected, or paroled into the United States by a U.S. Immigration Official.

ARREST DATA: Subject was apprehended walking in the brush on the Cage Ranch in the vicinity of the single-metal pole line. Subject was not in possession of any immigration documents and admitted to being present in the United States illegally.

TRAVEL DATA: The above subject states that he left his home in Peru on or about September 10, 2004. Subject stated that he traveled by train from his home in Peru to the Peru/Guatemala border. Subject states that he entered Guatemala legally by use of a permit, although it became lost during his travels. Subject continued to travel through Guatemala by bus and arrived at the Guatemala/Mexico border on or about September 17, 2004. He illegally entered Mexico on or about September 18, 2004, by walking. Subject traveled through Mexico by train and on foot until reaching Reynosa, Tamaulipas, Mexico on October 14, 2004. The subject stated that he entered illegally into the United States on October 15, 2004. Once in Reynosa, Tamaulipas, Mexico, he and other people walked for about one day through the brush until reaching an unknown house. Once there, all subjects entered a vehicle and were transported to an undisclosed location south of the Falfurrias, Texas Border Patrol Checkpoint. All of the passengers exited the vehicle and were then guided through the brush for about three days until being apprehended by Border Patrol Agents.

PURPOSE FOR ENTRY: Subject stated that he entered the United States in order to seek employment in Davis, California.

RECORD CHECKS: KAK960 was contacted and all Record Checks were NEGATIVE on the subject.

CREDIBLE FEAR: Subject stated that he does not fear returning to Peru.

DETENTION SPACE: Camp space was denied by SIEA Perez at 1330 due to lack of available space.

DISPOSITION: Subject was issued a Notice To Appear before an Immigration Judge on

Signature	Title
RODOLFO MORENO	BORDER PATROL AGENT

____2____ of ___3___ Pages

Form I-831 Continuation Page (Rev. 6/12/92)

Alien's Name	File Number Case No: FLF0510000363	Date
███████████████		10/19/2004

November 19, 2004 at 1:00 p.m. in Los Angeles, California.

It was explained to the subject the importance of reporting to the Immigration Judge on the scheduled time and Date. Subject was also warned that failing to report to his hearing would result in him being deported in absentia and a warrant issued for his arrest.

Signature RODOLFO MORENO	Title BORDER PATROL AGENT

___3___ of ___3___ Pages

Form I-831 Continuation Page (Rev. 6/12/92)

TAB 'M':

DHS Motion to Change Venue

Office of the Chief Counsel
Immigration and Customs Enforcement
United States Department of Homeland Security
606 South Olive Street, 8th Floor
Los Angeles, California 90014
(213) 894-2805

EXECUTIVE OFFICE FOR IMMIGRATION REVIEW
UNITED STATES DEPARTMENT OF JUSTICE
LOS ANGELES, CALIFORNIA

In the Matter of	)	UNITED STATES DEPARTMENT
	)	OF HOMELAND SECURITY'S
████████████████████	)	MOTION TO CHANGE VENUE
	)	
██████████	)	
	)	
In Removal Proceedings	)	
	)	

The United States Department of Homeland Security moves to change the venue of the above-mentioned case to San Francisco, California. 8 C.F.R. § 1003.20(b) (2007).

The respondent resides in Davis, California, which is located within the jurisdiction of the immigration court in San Francisco. As a result, good cause exists to transfer the respondent's case. 8 C.F.R. § 1003.20(b); *Matter of Rahman*, 20 I&N Dec. 480 (BIA 1992). The respondent would not be prejudiced by a change of venue to San Francisco, as he resides nearer to the immigration court in that city than he does to the immigration court in Los Angeles.

For the aforementioned reason, the Department requests that the immigration court grant its motion and change the venue of this case to San Francisco, California.

June 23, 2008   Respectfully submitted,

                                                     Kristin Piepmeier
                                                     Assistant Chief Counsel

CERTIFICATE OF SERVICE

I hereby certify that I have sent a copy of the attached document(s) via regular mail to:

[REDACTED]

8 C.F.R. § 1003.32(a).

Dated: 6/23/08

Kristin Piepmeier
Assistant Chief Counsel

TAB 'N':

Notice of Hearing Dated July 7, 2008 and Proof of USPS Return to Sender

NOTICE OF HEARING IN REMOVAL PROCEEDINGS
IMMIGRATION COURT
606 SOUTH OLIVE ST., 15TH FL.
LOS ANGELES, CA 90014

RE:
FILE:

DATE: Jul 7, 2008

TO:

Please Go to
14th Floor, Courtroom G

Please take notice that the above captioned case has been scheduled for a MASTER hearing before the Immigration Court on Jul 25, 2008 at 08:30 A.M. at:
606 SOUTH OLIVE ST., 15TH FL.
LOS ANGELES, CA, 90014

You may be represented in these proceedings, at no expense to the Government, by an attorney or other individual who is authorized and qualified to represent persons before an Immigration Court. Your hearing date has not been scheduled earlier than 10 days from the date of service of the Notice to Appear in order to permit you the opportunity to obtain an attorney or representative. If you wish to be represented, your attorney or representative must appear with you at the hearing prepared to proceed. You can request an earlier hearing in writing.

Failure to appear at your hearing except for exceptional circumstances may result in one or more of the following actions: (1) You may be taken into custody by the Department of Homeland Security and held for further action. OR (2) Your hearing may be held in your absence under section 240(b)(5) of the Immigration and Nationality Act. An order of removal will be entered against you if the Department of Homeland Security established by clear, unequivocal and convincing evidence that a) you or your attorney has been provided this notice and b) you are removable.

IF YOUR ADDRESS IS NOT LISTED ON THE NOTICE TO APPEAR, OR IF IT IS NOT CORRECT, WITHIN FIVE DAYS OF THIS NOTICE YOU MUST PROVIDE TO THE IMMIGRATION COURT LOS ANGELES, CA THE ATTACHED FORM EOIR-33 WITH YOUR ADDRESS AND/OR TELEPHONE NUMBER AT WHICH YOU CAN BE CONTACTED REGARDING THESE PROCEEDINGS. EVERYTIME YOU CHANGE YOUR ADDRESS AND/OR TELEPHONE NUMBER, YOU MUST INFORM THE COURT OF YOUR NEW ADDRESS AND/OR TELEPHONE NUMBER WITHIN 5 DAYS OF THE CHANGE ON THE ATTACHED FORM EOIR-33. ADDITIONAL FORMS EOIR-33 CAN BE OBTAINED FROM THE COURT WHERE YOU ARE SCHEDULED TO APPEAR. IN THE EVENT YOU ARE UNABLE TO OBTAIN A FORM EOIR-33, YOU MAY PROVIDE THE COURT IN WRITING WITH YOUR NEW ADDRESS AND/OR TELEPHONE NUMBER BUT YOU MUST CLEARLY MARK THE ENVELOPE "CHANGE OF ADDRESS." CORRESPONDENCE FROM THE COURT, INCLUDING HEARING NOTICES, WILL BE SENT TO THE MOST RECENT ADDRESS YOU HAVE PROVIDED, AND WILL BE CONSIDERED SUFFICIENT NOTICE TO YOU AND THESE PROCEEDINGS CAN GO FORWARD IN YOUR ABSENCE.

A list of free legal service providers has been given to you. For information regarding the status of your case, call toll free 1-800-898-7180 or 703-305-1662.

CERTIFICATE OF SERVICE
THIS DOCUMENT WAS SERVED BY: MAIL [ ] PERSONAL SERVICE (P)
TO: [ ] ALIEN [ ] ALIEN c/o Custodial Officer [ ] ALIEN's ATT/REP [ ] DHS
DATE: 7/7/08 BY: COURT STAFF _____ Z3
Attachments [ ] EOIR-33 [ ] EOIR-28 [ ] Legal Services List [ ] Other

NIXIE   957   CC 1   77 07/16/08

RETURN TO SENDER
NOT DELIVERABLE AS ADDRESSED
UNABLE TO FORWARD

BC: 90014185115   *0052-00700-07-40

TAB 'O':

Notice of Hearing Dated July 25, 2008 and Proof of USPS Return to Sender

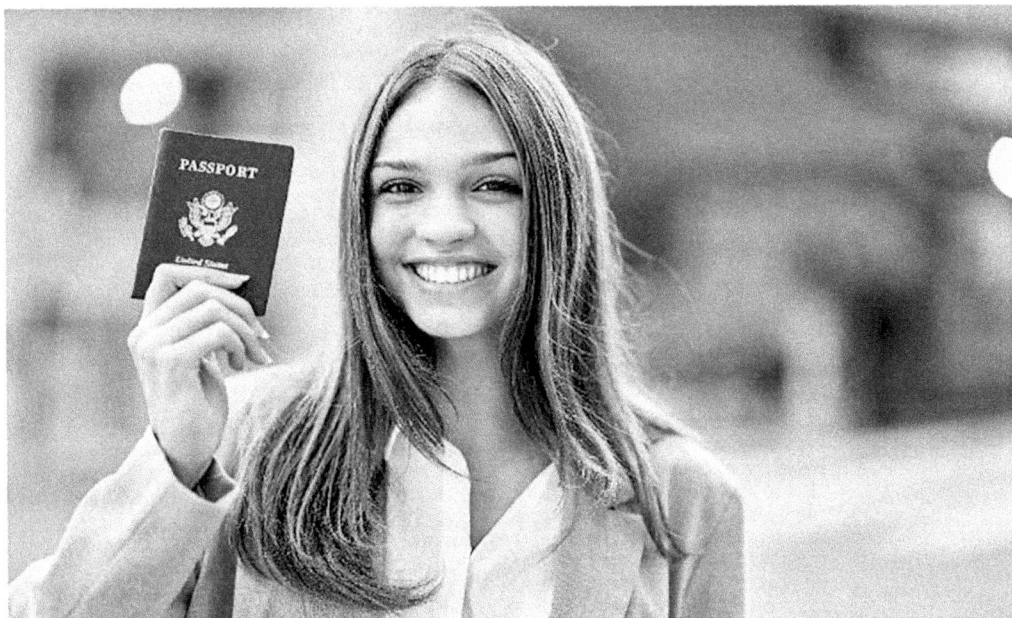

NOTICE OF HEARING IN REMOVAL PROCEEDINGS
IMMIGRATION COURT
606 SOUTH OLIVE ST., 15TH FL.
LOS ANGELES, CA 90014

RE: ████████████████████████
FILE: 098-350-736

DATE: Jul 25, 2008

TO: ████████████████████████

**Please Go to
14th Floor, Courtroom G**

Please take notice that the above captioned ████████████████████████
MASTER hearing before the Immigration Court on Oct 17, 2008 at 09:00 A.M. at:
606 SOUTH OLIVE ST., 15TH FL.
LOS ANGELES, CA, 90014

You may be represented in these proceedings, at no expense to the
Government, by an attorney or other individual who is authorized and qualified
to represent persons before an Immigration Court. Your hearing date has not
been scheduled earlier than 10 days from the date of service of the Notice to
Appear in order to permit you the opportunity to obtain an attorney or
representative. If you wish to be represented, your attorney or representative
must appear with you at the hearing prepared to proceed. You can request an
earlier hearing in writing.

Failure to appear at your hearing except for exceptional circumstances
may result in one or more of the following actions: (1) You may be taken into
custody by the Department of Homeland Security and held for further
action. OR (2) Your hearing may be held in your absence under section 240(b)(5)
of the Immigration and Nationality Act. An order of removal will be entered
against you if the Department of Homeland Security established by
clear, unequivocal and convincing evidence that a) you or your attorney has
been provided this notice and b) you are removable.

IF YOUR ADDRESS IS NOT LISTED ON THE NOTICE TO APPEAR, OR IF IT IS NOT
CORRECT, WITHIN FIVE DAYS OF THIS NOTICE YOU MUST PROVIDE TO THE IMMIGRATION
COURT LOS ANGELES, CA THE ATTACHED FORM EOIR-33 WITH YOUR ADDRESS AND/OR
TELEPHONE NUMBER AT WHICH YOU CAN BE CONTACTED REGARDING THESE PROCEEDINGS.
EVERYTIME YOU CHANGE YOUR ADDRESS AND/OR TELEPHONE NUMBER, YOU MUST INFORM THE
COURT OF YOUR NEW ADDRESS AND/OR TELEPHONE NUMBER WITHIN 5 DAYS OF THE CHANGE
ON THE ATTACHED FORM EOIR-33. ADDITIONAL FORMS EOIR-33 CAN BE OBTAINED FROM
THE COURT WHERE YOU ARE SCHEDULED TO APPEAR. IN THE EVENT YOU ARE UNABLE TO
OBTAIN A FORM EOIR-33, YOU MAY PROVIDE THE COURT IN WRITING WITH YOUR NEW
ADDRESS AND/OR TELEPHONE NUMBER BUT YOU MUST CLEARLY MARK THE ENVELOPE "CHANGE
OF ADDRESS." CORRESPONDENCE FROM THE COURT, INCLUDING HEARING NOTICES, WILL BE
SENT TO THE MOST RECENT ADDRESS YOU HAVE PROVIDED, AND WILL BE CONSIDERED
SUFFICIENT NOTICE TO YOU AND THESE PROCEEDINGS CAN GO FORWARD IN YOUR ABSENCE.

A list of free legal service providers has been given to you. For
information regarding the status of your case, call toll free 1-800-898-7180
or 703-305-1662.

CERTIFICATE OF SERVICE
THIS DOCUMENT WAS SERVED BY: MAIL (M) PERSONAL SERVICE (P)
TO: [ ] ALIEN [ ] ALIEN c/o Custodial Officer [ ] ALIEN's ATT/REP [ ] DHS
DATE: 7/25/08 BY: COURT STAFF _____ Z3
Attachments: [ ] EOIR-33 [ ] EOIR-28 [ ] Legal Services List [ ] Other

$ 00.42

NIXIE   957   CE 1   77   07/31/08

RETURN TO SENDER
NOT DELIVERABLE AS ADDRESSED
UNABLE TO FORWARD

BC: 90014162099   *0962-06959-25-43

SE61834970 R009
90014Q1623

UNITED STATES DEPARTMENT OF JUSTICE
EXECUTIVE OFFICE FOR IMMIGRATION REVIEW
IMMIGRATION COURT
606 SOUTH OLIVE ST., 15TH FL.
LOS ANGELES, CA 90014

IN THE MATTER OF   FILE A ▓▓▓▓▓   DATE: Oct 17, 2008
MEZA-AVENIO, AMERICO ERNESTO

___ UNABLE TO FORWARD - NO ADDRESS PROVIDED

___ ATTACHED IS A COPY OF THE DECISION OF THE IMMIGRATION JUDGE. THIS DECISION
IS FINAL UNLESS AN APPEAL IS FILED WITH THE BOARD OF IMMIGRATION APPEALS
WITHIN 30 CALENDAR DAYS OF THE DATE OF THE MAILING OF THIS WRITTEN DECISION.
SEE THE ENCLOSED FORMS AND INSTRUCTIONS FOR PROPERLY PREPARING YOUR APPEAL.
YOUR NOTICE OF APPEAL, ATTACHED DOCUMENTS, AND FEE OR FEE WAIVER REQUEST
MUST BE MAILED TO: BOARD OF IMMIGRATION APPEALS
                  OFFICE OF THE CLERK
                  P.O. BOX 8530
                  FALLS CHURCH, VA 22041

_X_ ATTACHED IS A COPY OF THE DECISION OF THE IMMIGRATION JUDGE AS THE RESULT
OF YOUR FAILURE TO APPEAR AT YOUR SCHEDULED DEPORTATION OR REMOVAL HEARING.
THIS DECISION IS FINAL UNLESS A MOTION TO REOPEN IS FILED IN ACCORDANCE
WITH SECTION 242B(c)(3) OF THE IMMIGRATION AND NATIONALITY ACT, 8 U.S.C.
SECTION 1252B(c)(3) IN DEPORTATION PROCEEDINGS OR SECTION 240(c)(6),
8 U.S.C. SECTION 1229a(c)(6) IN REMOVAL PROCEEDINGS. IF YOU FILE A MOTION
TO REOPEN, YOUR MOTION MUST BE FILED WITH THIS COURT:

                  IMMIGRATION COURT
                  606 SOUTH OLIVE ST., 15TH FL.
                  LOS ANGELES, CA 90014

___ OTHER: _____

                             COURT CLERK
                             IMMIGRATION COURT   FF

    CC:

TAB 'P':

Decision of the Immigration Judge

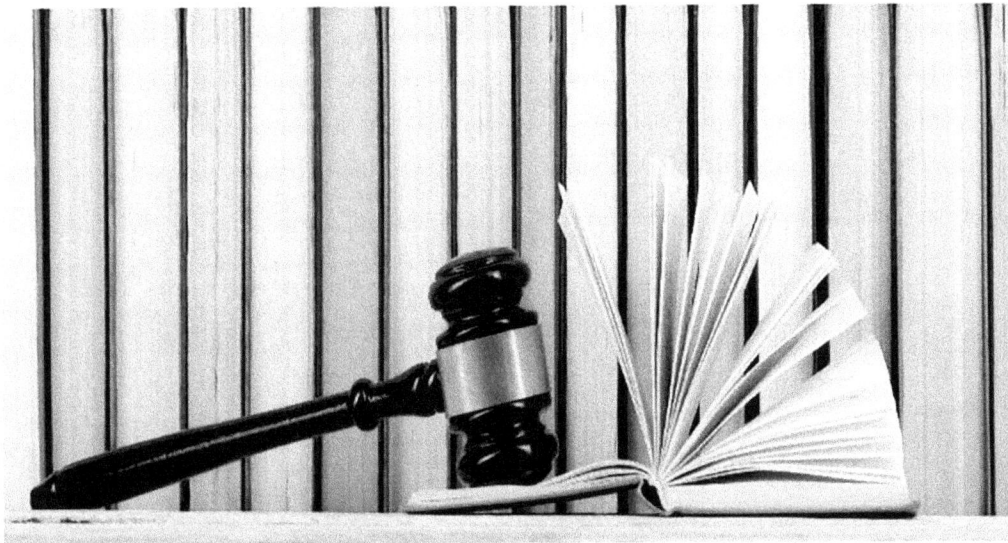

IN THE MATTER OF:

DATE: Oct 17, 2008

CASE NO.

RESPONDENT IN REMOVAL PROCEEDINGS

DECISION

Jurisdiction was established in this matter by the filing of the Notice to Appear issued by the Department of Homeland Security, with the Executive Office for Immigration Review and by service upon the respondent. See 8 C.F.R. § 1003.14(a), 103.5a.

The respondent was provided written notification of the time, date and location of the respondent's removal hearing. The respondent was also provided a written warning that failure to attend this hearing, for other than exceptional circumstances, would result in the issuance of an order of removal in the respondent's absence provided that removability was established. Despite the written notification provided, the respondent failed to appear at his/her hearing, and no exceptional circumstances were shown for his/her failure to appear. This hearing was, therefore, conducted in absentia pursuant to section 240(b)(5)(A) of the Immigration and Nationality Act.

[ ]   At a prior hearing the respondent admitted the factual allegations in the Notice to Appear and conceded removability. I find removability established as charged.

[X]   The Department of Homeland Security submitted documentary evidence relating to the respondent which established the truth of the factual allegations contained in the Notice to Appear. I find removability established as charged.

I further find that the respondent's failure to appear and proceed with any applications for relief from removal constitutes an abandonment of any pending applications and any applications the respondent may have been eligible to file. Those applications are deemed abandoned and denied for lack of prosecution. See Matter of Pearson, 13 I&N Dec. 152 (BIA 1969); Matter of Perez, 19 I&N Dec. 433 (BIA 1987); Matter of R-R, 20 I&N Dec. 547 (BIA 1992).

ORDER: The respondent shall be removed to PERU or in the alternative to on the charge(s) contained in the Notice to Appear.

_____
JOHN F. WALSH
Immigration Judge

cc: Assistant District Counsel
     Attorney for Respondent/Respondent

Z1

TAB 'Q':

Google Results for 3110 Nantucket Terrace, Davis, CA 95616

78 | P a g e

... the State of Michigan, the State of **California** or the State of Illinois (and such 1
21520 WATERS DISCOVERY **TERRACE** 7.500 2,166.52 80 7,250 2,166.52 ......
1,919.55 365,290.00 **DAVIS CA** 95616 1 11/24/98 00 5480652 05 01/01/99 0 ......
148,000.00 ZZ 360 147,567.79 1 3435 **NANTUCKET DRIVE** 7 500 1,034 84 ...

*In order to show you the most relevant results, we have omitted some
entries very similar to the 8 already displayed.
If you like, you can repeat the search with the omitted results included.*

United States Department of Justice
Executive Office for Immigration Review
Immigration Court
Los Angeles, California

In the Matter of:

A▉ ▉

ORDER OF THE IMMIGRATION JUDGE

Upon consideration of Respondent's Motion to Reopen, Motion to Rescind In Absentia Order of Removal and Automatic Stay of Removal, it is HEREBY ORDERED that the motion be
[ ] **GRANTED** [ ] **DENIED** because:

    [ ] DHS does not oppose the motion.
    [ ] Respondent does not oppose the motion.
    [ ] A response to the motion has not been filed with the Court.
    [ ] Good case has been established for the motion.
    [ ] The Court agrees with the reasons stated in the opposition to the motion.
    [ ] The motion is untimely per _____.
    [ ] Other:

Deadlines:

    [ ] The application (s) for relief must be filed by _____.
    [ ] Respondent must comply with DHS biometrics instructions by _____.

_____
Date

_____
Immigration Judge

_____
Certificate of Service

This document was served by: _____ Mail _____ Personal Service
To: [ ] Alien [ ] Alien c/o Custodial Officer [ ] Alien's Atty/Rep [ ] DHS
Date: _____ By: Court Staff: _____

CERTIFICATE OF SERVICE

I, Christopher A. Reed, hereby certify that I am a resident of or employed in the County of Los Angeles, over 18 years of age, not a party to the within action and that I am employed at and my business address is:

Law Offices of Brian D. Lerner, APC
3233 E. Broadway
Long Beach, CA 90803
Telephone: (562) 495-0554
Facsimile: (562) 608-8672

On April 24, 2015, I served a copy of the attached *MOTION TO REOPEN, MOTION TO RESCIND IN ABSENTIA ORDER OF REMOVAL AND AUTOMATIC STAY OF REMOVAL* on the following person(s) by the method(s) indicated:

Office of the Chief Counsel
Department of Homeland Security
606 S. Olive Street, 8th Floor
Los Angeles, CA 90014
(Personal Service)

I declare under penalty of perjury that the foregoing is true and correct. Executed in Long Beach, California.

DATED: April 24, 2015   By: _____
                                             Christopher A. Reed
                                             Attorney at Law

ABOUT THE AUTHOR

Brian D. Lerner is an Immigration Lawyer and runs a National Immigration Law Firm for nearly 30 years. He is an attorney who is a certified specialist that might help in Immigration & Nationality Law as issued by the California State Bar, Board of Legal Specialization. Attorney Lerner is an expert in Immigration Law, Removal and Deportation, Citizenship, Waiver and Appeals.

He has been a licensed attorney since 1992 and started the Law Offices of Brian D. Lerner, APC. The immigration practice consists of Immigration and Nationality Law, and everything involved with and regarding immigration which includes citizenship, investment visas, family and employment visas, removal and deportation hearings, appeals, waivers, adjustment, consulate processing and all types of immigration and citizenship matters.

He has represented clients from all over the U.S. and in many countries around the world. One side of his practice is dedicated to keeping people in the U.S. and fighting for their immigration rights, while another side is to get people back who have been deported and removed from the U.S.

Also, there is the affirmative part of Immigration Law which Brian Lerner has helped numerous people come into the U.S. on business visas, investment visas, student visas, fiancée and marriage visas, religious visas and many more. Attorney Lerner has helped immigrants who are victims of crime and domestic violence or ones that are married to abusers.

In other words, Attorney Lerner has a firm that helps people all over the U.S. He has dedicated significant time to preparing numerous petitions and applications for you to get at a fraction of the price of hiring an attorney. He says it is the next best thing to a real attorney because they are real petitions prepared by an expert.

www.ingramcontent.com/pod-product-compliance
Lightning Source LLC
Chambersburg PA
CBHW051800200326
41597CB00025B/4629